I0881101

Praise for **Best Scar Wins**

"*Best Scar Wins* is a fun-to-read, fast-paced adventure you won't want to put down. Most importantly, it shows that running can save lives. I always say, *My best accomplishment is my next one.* After reading Matt's book, I'm inspired to do just that—and so will you!"

– Dave McGillivray, Race Director, the Boston Marathon, and Founder and President, DMSE Sports, Inc.

"Matt's leadership and his amazing story in this book set a high bar for the rest of us, but his message is universal: You can rise to most any challenge if you approach life with a mix of humility, gratitude, and steely determination. He leads by example, and the results are astonishing."

– Ned Brooks, Founder, National Kidney Donation Organization

"Matt didn't have to give his kidney. He chose to. Then he chose to do something even harder. This story is what selflessness and grit look like—rewriting what one human can do. I was there. I saw it. You need to read it."

– John Bezou, Head Run Coach, Hypoxia Performance, and Racing the Planet Grand Slam Plus Finisher

"In *Best Scar Wins*, Matt Cavanaugh brilliantly lends a novelist's voice to his hard-won lessons from a life of military service and elite endurance racing."

– August Cole, Coauthor, *Ghost Fleet*

"There are so many deep lessons to be learned from having a successful military career, from the beautiful sport of running, and from opening yourself up (or having say, a doctor do this), and donating a kidney to someone in need.

In each of Matt Cavanaugh's vulnerable anecdotes, there is the motivation, a story from his military exploits embedded with a lesson transferable to everyone—and not just elite runners, career military folks, or kidney donors, but literally everyone—or a story from one of the four desert races he did to raise awareness about the promise of kidney donation, and perhaps most poignantly, a profound sense of gratitude for being able to give in the spirit of 'radical generosity.'

Best Scar Wins isn't about competition, it's about allowing your scars—be they mental, emotional, or physical—to remind you of where you have been, the wisdom earned, the strength you exuded, and the potential that you have right now to face and endure any battle that awaits. It is also about the ripple effect of radical generosity. One person gives, and we all benefit from it in some way.

This is a necessary read for any human being embarking upon being better, more generous, and more filled with gratitude for the lives we get to live, and the challenges we get to face."

– Mirna Valerio, Author, *A Beautiful Work in Progress*

BEST SCAR WINS

Also by ML Cavanaugh

Strategy Strikes Back: How Star Wars *Explains Modern Military Conflict* (with John Amble, Max Brooks, and Jaym Gates)

Winning Westeros: How Game of Thrones *Explains Modern Military Conflict* (with John Amble, Max Brooks, and Jaym Gates)

BEST SCAR WINS

How You Can Be More Than You Were Before

ML CAVANAUGH

MATT HOLT

Matt Holt Books
An Imprint of BenBella Books, Inc.
Dallas, TX

Matt Holt is an imprint of BenBella Books, Inc.
8080 N. Central Expressway
Suite 1700
Dallas, TX 75206
benbellabooks.com
Send feedback to feedback@benbellabooks.com

BenBella and *Matt Holt* are federally registered trademarks.

Printed in the United States of America
10 9 8 7 6 5 4 3 2 1

Library of Congress Control Number: 2025024304
ISBN 9781637747742 (hardcover)
ISBN 9781637747759 (electronic)

Editing by Katie Dickman
Copyediting by Scott Calamar
Proofreading by Jenny Bridges and Rebecca Maines
Text design and composition by Jordan Koluch
Cover design by Morgan Carr
Cover photography by Sam Fanshawe
Interior photography credits: RacingThePlanet/Thiago Diz (all photos from the Namib Race, Atacama Crossing, and Antarctica); RacingThePlanet/Carlos Garcia Prieto (all photos from the Georgia Race)
Printed by Lake Book Manufacturing

For my two pūkekos

Contents

Foreword by Dean Karnazes	xiii
Author's Note	xv
Introduction: **The Things I Carried**	1
Chapter One: **That Others May Live**	11
Chapter Two: **Fortune Favors the Bold**	33
Chapter Three: **Murphy's Law**	45
Chapter Four: **No Plan Survives Contact** Race Across the Oldest Desert—The Namib	53
Chapter Five: **Shoot the Wolf Closest to the Sled**	85
Chapter Six: **Iron Sharpens Iron** Race Across the Muddiest Desert—The Caucasus	97
Chapter Seven: **You Can't Shoot a Cannon from a Canoe**	129
Chapter Eight: **Nobody Slays Dragons Alone** Race Across the Driest Desert—The Atacama	141

Chapter Nine: **Choose the Harder Right Over the Easier Wrong** 167

Chapter Ten: **Through Endurance We Conquer** 177

Race Across the Last Desert—Antarctica

Epilogue: **Best Scar Wins** 207

For Potential Kidney Donors 215

Acknowledgments 217

Non sibi sed aliis

Foreword

It's been said that a gift of money is valuable, whilst a gift of time invaluable. But Lieutenant Colonel (retired) Matt Cavanaugh went even further and gave a gift of life. Literally. A body part.

Such charity is unimaginable to most, but to Matt a dutiful calling compelled him to donate a kidney to another.

To whom? A family member? A brother, sister, or perhaps close cousin? That would be the conventional expectation, but Matt is anything but conventional. He gave this vital organ to a complete stranger.

Such selfless acts define people; they become lifetime cornerstones in which one's identity becomes indelibly fixed. A pinnacle testament of one's exceptional character.

Matt ascended convention in many more ways than one. Not only did he donate a kidney to a complete stranger, he set out to conquer one of the world's most daunting endurance events, the 4 Deserts Challenge, post organ donation. In thus attempting he hoped to demonstrate that not only could a person give the gift of life, they could continue living life to its fullest even after doing so.

What follows is an epic tale of discovery, determination, and heroism. *Best Scar Wins* is a raw and revealing story that obliterates preconceived notions of what is and isn't possible. Matt takes on an unforgettable journey, one that leaves us awed and uplifted and forever restores our belief in the magnificence of the human spirit.

Dean Karnazes
New York Times Bestselling Author,
Ultramarathon Man: Confessions of an All-Night Runner

Author's Note

I have attempted, where possible, to present this book in chronological order based on contemporaneous personal notes. However, there are instances where I've taken minor liberties with the timeline for narrative consistency. In places I have simplified conversations into single scenes that actually evolved over longer periods of time. This compression is in service to you, the reader, to make the story easier to understand.

With those modest adjustments for clarity—as crazy as this story gets—it is true. The donation, the races, the losses, the win. All of it.

I have the scars to prove it.

Introduction

THE THINGS I CARRIED

You may not see it when you hit rock bottom, but you sure can feel it.

May 3, 2022
Namib Desert, Namibia

It all began when I signed a lethal liability waiver.

> "The 4 Deserts Race Series and RacingThePlanet Ultra are 250-kilometer [155-mile] footraces that take place in some of the most extreme and hostile environments in the world. There are medical risks associated with taking part in these races . . . The list below includes some of the risks."

Then they made us check each block.

"Heat stroke." Check.

"Dehydration." Check.

"Kidney failure." Check.

That last one felt aimed at me. Like they wanted to scare me and my one remaining kidney off. Maybe it should have. Because at this moment—months later, on the third day of RacingThePlanet's Namib

Race—I questioned if I had made a terrible mistake, as I worried my one kidney might fail and I could die.

I also remember thinking while lying on the ground, *They're pulling my shoes off.*

One got stuck, and Dudu,[1] the Israeli ex–special forces guy, gave it a hard pull. Both it and the stubborn sock finally gave way.

I looked up and recognized Reinhold from Switzerland, who, along with Dudu, had finished just ahead of me. As I moved my lips to say something, a pitcher of water coated my face and obscured my vision. The water was warm, but the air all around me was hotter.

Dudu pours a pitcher of water on me at the end of Stage 3 in the Namib Race. Look pretty good, don't I?

I hadn't felt heat like that since I'd gotten off the plane for my first deployment to Iraq in 2003. "Holy cow, we've got fifty-five! Fifty-five Celsius! One hundred thirty-one Fahrenheit!" said Sam Fanshawe, the

1 A common Israeli nickname for "Daniel."

race director. But she didn't have to tell me. Like a frog, I was the last to figure out that I was the one in the boiling pot. When I finally realized, everything burned.

I tried to reorient and steady myself, but the heat made me woozy. My hands felt weird, like I'd borrowed someone else's fingers. My feet tingled and I couldn't balance myself to stand. I mostly gave in to the commands of the people who took my shoes and soaked me, because at least I wasn't so far gone that I couldn't recognize who knew best. My lone objection was to remain upright. They kept trying to lay me on the ground with my back flat and incline my legs. But that legs-above-the-heart position somehow made me even woozier, so I frowned and waved for them to leave me be.

I sat for hours facing that finish line to let my body cool down and my mind catch up.

The Namib Race is run across the Namib Desert in six self-supported stages. The basic race format—for the Namib and each of the 4 Deserts races—is that the first four stages are around twenty-five miles each, then The Long March is roughly fifty miles, and the final stage is about five miles to finish off the week. "Self-supported" means you carry everything you need for the week while running, including food, clothes, gear, sleeping necessities, and water. My too-heavy pack loaded with all my stuff, as much as the extreme heat, was why I was forced to sit and rest for the next several hours on a tarp in the middle of the world's oldest desert. This was no ordinary race, and it was only the first of the 4 Deserts Grand Slam series.

More runners soon joined my little island of exhaustion. Vicki, a British woman who would later win the women's division, came in not long after I did. She was one of the toughest, best prepared runners I'd ever met, and I wanted to say something to her, but I still wasn't able to speak. Part of it was embarrassment, because like many of us out there, I didn't want to feel like I'd lost control. No matter the heat and heavy pack and hundreds-of-miles-more-to-run situation.

But Vicki helped me rejoin the human race after my silent phase ended. We chatted about everything unrelated to the predicament we found ourselves in. Mostly food, because halfway through race week we were starved, burning thousands and thousands of calories daily, with far less than that to replace what had been lost.

"If we were in a pub, what would you order right now?" Vicki asked.

"Fish and chips. And then again. Then again," I responded automatically. Her British accent sealed it—all I could think about was salty, vinegar-soaked fries.

"Hey, what happened to your sock?" She noticed my one bare foot.

"Uh . . . I had it when I finished—obviously—and then I guess I lost it. I have no idea how you lose a sock at a race, but I just did."

We laughed. At least I still had both shoes.

Sam, the race director, came back over to brief those of us who had finished. "We're shutting down, halting anyone who still hasn't hit the last checkpoint. From that point on they'll get a truck ride in and be awarded a standard time for that last section they'll miss. It's too hot to race."

She went on to confirm the measured heat was way over the race's safe limit (set at 50 degrees Celsius, 122 degrees Fahrenheit).[2] One runner, an experienced 4 Deserts competitor, couldn't pee, an indicator that his kidneys couldn't function. He withdrew, along with one-fourth of the runners that started the race.

This heat mattered so much to me now because seven months earlier, against my wife's wishes, I had donated my left kidney at Walter Reed

2 It's a reasonable policy. "The physical consequences of competing in hot weather can range from cramps and dizziness to sudden death. Exertional heat stroke (EHS) occurs when a body overheats during strenuous activity and can lead to seizures and organ failure. The mortality rate for people hospitalized with EHS hovers around 15%; untreated it may be 80%." See "Hotter, harder, deadlier," *The Economist* (Sept. 14, 2024), 51.

National Military Medical Center. My donation, which went to a stranger in Seattle, kick-started a chain of transplants that would help another seven recipients, the final kidney going to someone back at Walter Reed.

Those runners that dropped became a sharp reminder of the harsh warning I'd gotten from one of America's most distinguished kidney doctors.[3] He told me not to race because it was too much stress too soon, that my one remaining kidney seven months after the donation was still taking on the functions of two—including filtering dangerous toxins from the blood and maintaining the balance and amount of salt and water in my body—both critical to desert running.

But I went ahead with the race because I wanted to be the first kidney donor to Grand Slam the world's toughest ultrarunning series.[4] I pitched the National Kidney Registry to support me in the attempt, and they green-lit me.

In that moment—sitting in the desert, exhausted and empty—that green light started blinking red.

At this point in the Namib, I had only done three stages of my Grand Slam year's planned twenty-four. So as bright and hot as that day was, my mind was in the deep dark. I would soon write to my wife that at this point, one of many low points, I felt "dark," an "intense blend of pain and sadness."

Maybe taking on this race seven months after surgery was too soon.

And this race was only the beginning. The 4 Deserts Grand Slam includes four events—in the Namib Desert, the Gobi Desert, the Atacama Desert, and across Antarctica—all at least as tough as the Namib. It would total 1,000 kilometers—620 miles—the distance from Sacramento

---

3 A nephrologist, in medical speak. Another transplant professional would later write, "I would have argued with you and adamantly told you not to race. The distance alone gives me pause but the heat of the desert is dangerous [for a recent kidney donor]."

4 Kidney donors (and interested parties) ought to discuss return-to-exercise protocols with their medical providers.

to Salt Lake, New York to Charlotte, Minneapolis to Detroit, or Tallahassee to the Texas state line. All of it with a pack carrying additional weight the rough equivalent of a toddler. Most years prior I had raced only a small fraction of that with nothing but clothes on my back.

Months later and an ocean away, at the end of Stage 3 in the Namib Desert, it all seemed so stupid. Like trying to hike up Mount Everest on a broken leg.

You may not see it when you hit rock bottom, but you sure can feel it. Every doubt you've ever had pours into the pit and drowns you.

I shouldn't have done this, I thought. *I'll have to pull out, and people will say, "Of course he couldn't make it, he's only got one kidney, his body couldn't handle the heat. He's short, he's weak, he's nothing special, another middle-middle-class kid from the middle of Minnesota. He's average, and average doesn't cut it in the desert."*

All these and more filled my mind—about the race, about how I'd gotten to Namibia. I didn't plan on any of this. I'd never done anything this big before. I felt too small to make it come true. It was supposed to be simple. One step, then another, then the next. But on that tarp, it felt like I might not have another step left in me.

I lost faith for a moment, but I still had all the things I carried.

The Namib Race required thirty-seven items, all inspectable pre-race and then again at any time during race week. They included:

A backpack. Waterproof bag. Sleeping bag. Headlamp. Red-flashing light. Multi-tool. Whistle. Mirror. Survival bivvy bag. Compass. Eating utensil. Two ounces of sunscreen. Lip balm (with sunscreen). Blister kit. Compression bandage. Medication (painkillers and for allergies). Safety pins. Alcohol gel (for cleaning hands, two ounces). Toilet paper. Running shoes. Socks. Tights/shorts. Run shirt. Warm long-sleeve top. Waterproof jacket. Rain poncho. Cap with neck cover. Warm hat. Gloves.

Sunglasses. Nationality patches. RacingThePlanet patches. Hydration system. Electrolytes/salt tablets. Face masks. Pre-race meals for camp. Minimum of 14,000 calories for seven days.

We were, of course, permitted to bring additional items for comfort, like a pad to sleep on and a player for music. Those added weight, but I brought them anyway.

All these items were important. But they weren't all I carried. I spent twenty-five years wearing a uniform, mostly as an award-winning military strategist and West Point professor, and along the way I picked up several slogans and sayings that were crucial to reaching so many finish lines. Many were there, planted in my head, as if from birth. They'd come naturally to mind, automatic like breathing. But others I had to think about, hold tight to—mantras and mottos for the toughest days. There were ten in all.

Along the way, on the hard road, another was born. The eleventh, an answer to the question about my kidney donation and races I've recited many times for many different people: "Matt, how did you do it?"

Three words explain everything: *Best scar wins.*

When I had nothing else left, I looked inside and I found more than simple strength in my scars—I found a superpower, a renewable resource waiting to be tapped. What's more, we all have scars, visible and invisible, and if we learn to see them differently, we can become more than we were before. Like most people, I am neither inherently great nor good. But in this tough year of racing I brought with me a compass (those ten insights) and locked on a North Star (*best scar wins*) that helped me find my way to a better place and a better me.

I want to pull these magnificent eleven out of my rucksack and put them into yours. I want to give them life, make them real, so they stick in your mind just as they've gotten glued into mine. In the chapters ahead, join me for races across seven months and four continents, weaving through challenges and checkpoints, and every so often we'll cross a chapter's finish line. Then we'll pause and reflect and do what the indomitable

Sir Winston Churchill did during the second World War. He would affix a red sticker with the words "ACTION THIS DAY" to his most urgent, must-do tasks. Those that must be accomplished (*Now!*) to move the great effort forward. In the same spirit, you'll draw lessons for actions this day to move your own great effort forward as well.

Because as bad as moments in the Namib went, I couldn't see then what I see now. That as awful as things would look, as far gone as I got, I could always reach in my rucksack for one of these lessons to solve one problem, then another, then the next. That was the way I worked through the hardest challenges I've ever encountered. One step at a time, each one guided by every lesson and experience, slogan and saying I picked up from my military career.

Each one of these unlocked another gear inside that got me up again and again and again, to find my own hidden Hercules when failure had its hot breath on my neck. This book puts these lessons up like ornaments on a tree—for you and others to pull down and put into practice.

Beyond teachable moments, I also didn't know what exceptional character—and characters—I'd get to meet during a global race spanning four continents. An incredibly tall, perpetually smiling former Polish *Ninja Warrior* competitor. A full-chest-tattooed ex-soldier from Great Britain who'd recently rowed alone across the Atlantic Ocean for 111 days. A speed demon nicknamed "Bilbo Baggins." A one-armed Norwegian woman who transformed a life of drug addiction into one of desert racing. An airline pilot and adventurer from Alaska who looked back from her cockpit to hear her flight attendant mention she needed a kidney, and then she gave her one of her own. A blind Brazilian runner who covered terrible terrain as well as any sighted person. The people I met at the 4 Deserts breathed oxygen into the cliché that truth really is stranger than fiction.

With these lessons and people, in mind and heart, somehow, over the seven months (214 days—yes, I counted) of my 4 Deserts Grand Slam year, I encountered a maelstrom of maladies, misadventures, and mistakes:

back-to-back cancelled international flights, a sandstorm, packs of pissed-off wild dogs, hailstorms, zero-visibility fog, a busted water bottle in oven-like desert heat, a terrible "Drake shake" crossing the world's worst sea to Antarctica, athletic tape that ripped flesh from my upper back, painful physical therapy, and far too many lost toenails to count.

And yet.

I made it. Across 1,000 kilometers of sand, mud, rock, and ice, I made it. With my fingernails at times, on all fours at times, always with one kidney.

Some will read my single kidney as a handicap. As in, "Wow, you did that *despite* having only one kidney."

It's the other way around. I did it *because* I have one kidney. Sometimes human greatness grows from human goodness.

So, after even more hours on that tarp in the Namib, the sun started to hang low. The heat dropped a bit. I finally stood up.

I scanned and saw my friend John Bezou. We nodded to one another. Both US Army veterans, we didn't even really have to say what we were both thinking: *Embrace the suck.*

I spotted my tent and bent down to pick up my pack. I saw something black peek out from under the tarp's edge.

My missing sock.

I picked it up, stepped off the tarp, and got ready for Stage 4.

Chapter One

THAT OTHERS MAY LIVE

One gift catalyzes many.

March 1, 2021
Manitou Springs, Colorado

"Hi, I'm Lieutenant Colonel Matt Cavanaugh. I'd like to donate my kidney."

A weird way to start a call. The enlisted soldier on the other end of the phone was confused. Not by what I'd said, but that in an organization full of checklists—Walter Reed National Military Medical Center—she didn't have one for this.

"I'm sorry, sir. I'll ask around. Someone will get back to you." The call went dead in under a minute.

In retrospect, it must have seemed like a prank. Why would a healthy officer want to give away a kidney?

But that's exactly why I had called. While I'd heard about living kidney donation long ago, I'd put a pin in the idea for many years. Then multiple converging personal reasons collided with the enormous number of Americans dying during the pandemic—death on a scale I just couldn't stomach—and on a slow work day I looked up the Army regulation on kidney donation. The bureaucratic document led me to a phone number for the transplant center at Walter Reed. So I lobbed them a call. The quick hang-up didn't give me much confidence in a callback.

A couple days later, early in the morning, Vilda did call. The head transplant nurse coordinator at Walter Reed rang me as I pulled on my shoes for my morning run.

I didn't recognize the number but picked up anyway.

A woman asked, "Is this Lieutenant Colonel Matthew Cavanaugh?"

"Speaking," I said.

"So you want to give away a kidney?" she said in a distinctly Caribbean accent.

What followed was a strangely straightforward talk about handing over a vital organ. I thought, *Huh, this actually doesn't sound so bad. Why not? Maybe I can fit this into September.*

We talked about it like scheduling a dental cleaning. By the time the call ended, I said I'd think about it and would be in touch soon.

My next thought was to tell Rachel.

Meeting her was all a glorious mistake.

In early 2009 I had gotten good enough at running that I was the All-Army Cross Country team's last pick for the National and Armed Force Cross Country Championships in Maryland. A young woman on my team told me she thought I'd be great for a friend of hers and asked me to message someone named Rachel on social media. (The "mistake" part: We later learned this teammate had never actually met Rachel, she only indirectly knew of her through Rachel's half sister.)

The little I knew was that Rachel lived in the Bay Area and was a principal dancer with the San Francisco Ballet, a high-level rank in the ballet world. I was nervous and thought it was more than a little odd to reach out to her that way, but I fired off the message anyway. Why not? I was moving a lot, focused on my military career, and didn't think much would come from a random referral to someone in San Fran.

Rachel wrote back a few days later, mentioned that she was definitely not single, was "working some things out with someone," and didn't want to lead me on. I told her "no worries," that I was "terribly fascinated" by her job, and, oh by the way, did she "know how intimidating it is to us guys that you're a ballerina?"

We wrote back and forth for a couple months, learning a little more and more about one another with each message.

At the same time, on a parallel track, a friend of mine at the military school I attended said she was going to visit San Francisco with some college friends. Having nothing to do that weekend, I said I'd tag along, that it sounded like fun. *After* I booked the flight, not wanting to impose or be weird, I told Rachel about my travel plans and wrote that "it would be nice to have a cup of coffee or something—actually meet you." She said yes.

The serendipity was stronger than we knew. My friend was going to visit a "college friend" who—unbeknownst to us—turned out to be Rachel's half sister (the very same one who had suggested that Rachel was single in the first place months before). So the group I intended to get together with was already to include Rachel.

Rachel and I had that coffee, with her half sister in tow (just in case I turned out to be a wacko, which, thankfully, I am not). Then we three walked to Mission Dolores, a gorgeous Spanish-era landmark in San Francisco. I had a camera with me, and my lens always seemed drawn to Rachel. I couldn't take my eyes off her then or the rest of the weekend.

It was somewhere between a juvenile crush and mature love. Probably both. I could see the contrasts from the start. Ballet left her balanced between a powerful athlete and a delicate soul. I was rougher at the edges; she was refined. I was a runner, violence in motion; she was elegant in movement. She was a garden rose; I was scrub oak. Beauty meets Beast. I hoped she'd overlook the underwhelming go-cart of a rental car I first picked her up in (at the time, she drove a sports car).

When Rachel offered me a ride back to Oakland Airport, I had to say something, even if I couldn't say the something I really wanted to say.

So I half went for it: "Rachel, this was really, really great. I had a lot of fun, and I want you to know that, if things were different, I would have liked to have asked you out on a real date."

We kept talking after that weekend. We moved from episodic messages to daily calls. A few weeks later I had to leave one military school in Arizona for another in Pennsylvania with ten days in between. I told Rachel that if we were going to see one another again, now would be the best time. She said yes, and I booked a ticket to fly back.

We dated, intensely, over the next days and weeks, compressed because we were both at major hinge points in life. Rachel was leaving the San Francisco Ballet; I was going school-to-school mid-military career.

In the Bay Area, we made the most of our limited time together. We held hands and walked Muir Woods, shared plates and private thoughts at Chez Panisse. When I made her laugh at dinner, she smiled, and I could've lived a full and content existence in her dimple. I wrote in my journal at the time "it was an amazing, life-changing week with Rachel." Heels above head.

We both felt the spark, and after a few months of talking and dating we'd danced around the subject enough that I drafted wedding vows, bought a ring, and—since she'd moved from the Bay Area to stay with family in Salt Lake City to figure out what would come next after the San Francisco Ballet—I flew to Utah see her for her birthday. I learned on arrival that she'd surprised me with a weekend at the Sundance Resort. When we got to our cabin, Rachel opened the door to the balcony and walked onto the deck. I followed.

"Your birthday gift," I said, as I handed her the Tiffany box wrapped in paper with my handwritten wedding vows on one side. As she read them, and approached the end, I dropped to one knee.

"Rachel, I love you with all my heart. Will you marry me?"

She said yes. It was the happiest moment of my life, and only the thirteenth day we'd spent in one another's physical presence. One month later, in July 2009, we went to a courthouse in Pennsylvania and were married. Our first daughter, Grace, came in 2011, and then another girl, Georgie, in 2014.

On one of those first dates in 2009, Rachel and I discussed the possibility of my donating a kidney. I told her then I might want to do it someday, and she had said, *OK, sure*—likely figuring it wouldn't come up again. We hadn't talked about it over the next dozen years, and then suddenly I resurrected the idea in early 2021.

We were on our house's elevated front porch, girls in the yard below us. "Honey, you remember I told you about donating a kidney?" I asked.

"Yeah . . . wait, you mean the thing you said you might want to do someday?" Rachel responded.

"I called the military hospital near DC, Walter Reed, about it, and I want to start the process. I don't know if I'd be cleared to donate, but I'd like to see if it's a possibility."

Rachel shrugged. She said, "Okay," paused, and then, "I know it's important to you. Why not."

We left it at that. Her body language betrayed a small shock, but considering the stage of life we were in—healthy, financially secure—I thought it was as good a time as any. I was fast approaching my military retirement in the next two years, and this felt like a final act of service before taking off the uniform for good.

The next day I searched the internet and found a recent kidney donor, athlete, and fellow West Point graduate four years my senior. Dave was a mountain climber and about to attempt the Seven Summits.[5] I figured if

5 To climb the seven highest points on the seven different continents, including Mount Everest.

this guy could donate a kidney (in addition to part of his liver) and then go on to tacklc big, bold adventures like the Seven Summits, then I could too. We spoke, and after I hung up the phone with him I thought, *I'm in.* I emailed Vilda and told her to start the paperwork.

There wasn't much to do for a while, outside of a hospital blood draw in late April. The pandemic was still on, and due to virus restrictions, hospital visits were rare. When I got home from my blood draw, Rachel and I had our first serious talk about whether I'd give away my kidney.

It went poorly.

It was as if, without exchanging many words on the subject, we had drifted to a bad place on sheer momentum.

"So you've already decided," Rachel said, challenging the step-by-step nature of the process. She pointed out that I was just going along from one appointment to the next as if it were all certain.

"I'm just doing what they tell me," I said defensively. "If I don't do these things, I won't be able to find out if I'm even able to go through with it." I tried to leave open the chance I might not be eligible, which we both knew was unlikely.

"What if something happens? It's not just you at risk. It's us. All of us."

She was right. I couldn't refute that. If something went wrong, it wouldn't be like a sniper's bullet that hit me and only me. It'd be a bomb spraying shrapnel on her and the girls too. I didn't know how to respond.

"Look, why should we argue about something that might be moot, might not even happen? If the tests find me good to go, then let's talk about it for real. But let's not fight over this, not now." We ended at a stalemate. It was just too hard, so we punted.

Vilda scheduled my physical for June 1 and 2. In the interim I did a few over-the-phone medical appointments, including with a psychologist and social worker. It turns out the medical profession asks a few extra questions when someone wants to donate a kidney to someone they've never met.

The social worker called while I was driving to work. I pulled over, parked the car, and spent an hour answering questions about life, work, my background, and: *Why this? Why now?* After talking around it for some time, he asked point-blank: "Why do you want to donate a kidney to a stranger?"

Earlier that week I had written a list of reasons why to donate and why not to go ahead with it. I gulped and just let it all out.

> Look, with a relatively low risk to myself, I get to save someone's life. I see that as a natural extension of my military career, which is that for my entire adult life I've been conditioned to risk and self-sacrifice for some greater good. For something more than myself. For others. That's why I've stayed in the Army as long as I have, and this is who I am now.

While I blurted it all out, I could still picture the medic who patched me up from a bad scrape during Cadet Basic Training at West Point. He'd been a US Air Force pararescuer before the Army, and he asked cadets to recite the pararescue motto on entry to his aid station: "That others may live."

But I wasn't only trying to live up to some military motto, however beautiful I thought it was. It was more that I was acutely aware that I'd tried and failed so many times to be of use to others. And I was fed up with what I couldn't do. I needed to find something I could do. Something that would work. Something good.

Kidney donation seemed like that good thing. The impact is usually immediate, undeniable, complete.

I acknowledged my worries about my family to the social worker. By far my only hesitation came from the risk to Rachel, Grace, and Georgie. It hurt to think that this might hurt them. But when I balanced that low probability potential against pulling someone out of true misery, even if a stranger to us, I was swayed to go forward. I told the social worker I had faith that, because Rachel was an exceptional mother—if the worst happened—I knew she'd find a great life for her and the girls after I was gone.

"Sorry to go on for so long." I apologized for speechifying.

"Wow," he said. "That is the most thoughtful response to that question I've ever heard, and I've been doing this for twenty-five years." It heartened me exactly when I needed it.

On May 31, I flew from Colorado Springs to Ronald Reagan Washington National Airport near Washington, DC.

The next morning, at 5 AM, I was awake and starving, but Vilda had warned me to skip food for all the lab work to come. After a short ride, the bus dropped me in front of the main hospital building. At 6:50 AM, I found Vilda at the front of the nephrology department.

"Matthew?" she said. We had never met in person. I smiled when I heard that familiar Caribbean accent, and I said, "Good morning, Vilda." She invited me back into an office.

She got straight to the point. She listed drawbacks, potential consequences from the surgical procedure, and then looked me right in the eye and asked: "Are you certain you want to do this?"

"Yes," I said.

We talked more about the tests to come. In eight years of testing, she had found two people who learned they had only one kidney to begin with and were therefore ineligible to donate. This fact—that many people are born with a single kidney, one in every few thousand—reinforced for me the idea that we can get along fine with just one kidney.

Vilda handed me a light-blue twenty-four-hour blood pressure monitor that I slid over my upper arm and walked me down to the lab for a blood test. I also picked up an orange milk-jug-sized bottle to collect my urine for the next day (to gauge total output volume).

Not long after, while I waited in front of the lab, I overheard two nurses talking about a little girl—she was right across the waiting area from me—who had just gotten a kidney from a living donor. Seeing a transplant recipient my own daughter's age hit like a stick to the heart. This was real.

But the approval process was strange. By 8 AM they had already taken twenty-three tiny vials of blood from my arm, I had sucked down a ten-ounce sugary, orange glucose drink, and watched a nineties-era video with an over-the-top, thick-accented, mustachioed older Italian guy who explained the basics of a "laparoscopic live donor nephrectomy."

From then on, rapid-fire tests: radiology and a chest X-ray, back to the lab for more blood work, cardiology for an EKG. In the process I learned how difficult wearing this twenty-four-hour blood pressure cuff was going to be.

It would fire every twenty minutes without warning. I would walk up to a desk where I needed a medical test. Someone would slide me a piece of paper. Then my blood pressure cuff would go off, seize up, force my arm to fully straighten out, rendering it useless. I became the intermittent one-armed man.

It got worse. I had to poop. I went to the bathroom, but when I sat down, I had to hold my orange jug with one hand between my knees in front of the toilet bowl and then use the other hand to aim my urine into the jug's quarter-sized hole. Midstream, the blood pressure cuff fired, and I had a millisecond to switch both the orange jug and my penis into one hand to keep the urine flowing into the jug (while my cuffed arm froze straight). Then "number two" came, along with lots of sweat. Miraculously, I caught everything that needed catching and let fly everything that needed flying. It easily made my top-ten Ridiculous Moments list (though not as high as you'd hope).

Next I had to climb into a giant metal donut (aka a CT scanner).

"Pants down, arms up. Keep that cuff out of the machine," the tech directed.

"I don't think I can all the way. My arms aren't that flexible," I said.

"Do your best. And heads up, when the dye goes in, you'll get a metallic taste and feel like peeing your pants. Try not to."

"Wait, huh?" But by then the giant donut woke up, got noisy, and flashed disco spurts of green, blue, purple, and yellow.

The dye injected into my IV line, which shot a warm sensation into me. I got the metallic taste (*check*, I thought) and felt like wetting my pants (*check*). Thankfully, I did not.

For lunch I wandered into the cafeteria. I took a tray and, again, out of total terror for the one-armed-man thing, put my partially full orange urine jug atop the tray in an effort to stabilize both the jug and the tray simultaneously. The employee at the counter looked at me, apparently not fazed at all by my jug, though he had to know what it was for, and asked, "Is that all?" referring to the food on the other half of the tray.

I paid and walked to an empty table.

Loneliness set in. I was done with the pre-spaceflight-level physical tests for the day, and all I had left to do was let the blood pressure cuff do its work and fill my urine jug. Just wait and think and shoot straight.

I did good. By the next morning at 8 AM, I turned in my orange jug with 2.1 liters of urine. Nearly five pounds of pale-yellow ale in twenty-four hours! I gave it to the basement lab guy, who grinned his approval.

Then Vilda and I met near the nephrology department, in the lobby where we'd seen the little girl kidney recipient.

"You're approved. You can donate," she told me.

"Wow, seriously?" I asked. "I guess this means my kidney's pretty hot, huh?"

"Ten out of ten, Matt, your kidney's a ten."

"So you think I'm beautiful on the inside?" I joked, thinking momentarily about my genetic lottery-winning combo of Tom Cruise's height and an Owen Wilsonesque nose.

Then I went serious and told her, "I want to set up a chain."

In the last couple decades, many transplant hospitals, connected by nonprofits, have applied math and logistics to maximize each kidney donation's benefits in what's known as a "chain donation." For example, it's common that someone wants to donate to a family member in need, but they are not suited to donate to them. Chain donations address that. Say Adam (type A blood) needs a kidney; his wife wants to donate but is type

B. Otto (type O) also needs a kidney; his wife is type A.[6] In cases like these, a chain of donations can help everybody. An altruistic donor with type O comes along and donates to Otto, and in exchange, Otto's wife donates to Adam, whose loved one in turn donates, and so on. The better the match, the longer the transplanted kidney likely lasts. These chains can play out over months and have resulted in as many as nearly three dozen transplants in a single sequence. One gift catalyzes many.

It's a high-stakes give-a-penny-take-a-penny system. But you need someone to put a penny in the tray to start. I wanted my kidney to be the first in the tray.

Vilda and I talked more about how important kidneys are, even at only the size of a fist. I had read some of the explanatory pamphlets in the waiting rooms. Kidneys filter dangerous toxins from our blood—the entire bloodstream gets filtered through the kidneys about two dozen times a day and they send on waste as urine. And when they fail, they tend to fail in pairs, which is what makes kidney transplants necessary; if people could rely on their second kidney as a "fail-safe," then almost no one would need a transplant.

But many do. Vilda told me just how prevalent this is. One in three Americans is at risk for kidney disease; more than 37 million have chronic kidney disease (most don't even know). At any given time, around 700,000 Americans are dying due to kidney failure. Of those, only about 100,000 are on a waiting list for transplant, including 1,000 children, and in most years about 5,000 to 6,000 on that list die waiting, hooked up to dialysis machines for hours and hours several days a week, waiting and hoping for a transplant. Living donation gets patients off that multiyear wait list.

"One more thing, Vilda," I told her. "I need to do this in mid-September.

---

6 Blood type is one of many ways of matching kidney donors to recipients and used here to simplify the far more comprehensive process, which includes genetic matching.

I have important work events in August, and I'd like to be healed up in time for ski season with my girls."

"I'll try, but it's not entirely up to me. We'll see," Vilda said.

I called Rachel to tell her the news that I'd been OK'd for surgery. She was in the yard with the kids, so in a good mood to hear it. Luckily.

What I didn't say on the phone, but only later recognized, was that this was the point beyond which there was no turning back. I had decided.

If I didn't go through with it, I wouldn't feel like me anymore. At this point I had full knowledge that if I didn't see this through, someone—probably several someones—would die. I couldn't get that thought out of my head.

It reminded me of when I would take Grace and Georgie with me when I donated blood. They mostly went for the snacks and soda, but they'd also stand beside me while the needle was in my arm. Once Grace asked, "Daddy, do you have any blood left?" Another time Georgie asked, "Daddy, after your blood gets to someone who needs it, how do they take it? Do they *drink* your blood?" Aside from the adorable anecdotes, I brought them to see that we don't fiddle while someone's Rome burns. We give of ourselves, whenever we can.

I wanted them to see that a radical sense of generosity isn't an obligation, but a privilege, an opportunity, not a hardship. That it's not only a good gesture but maybe a drop of water in the bucket for when our own Rome burns. I thought the same about kidney donation. I wanted the kids, someday, to know what Daddy would do for someone else.

I also thought: *Maybe not now, but Rachel will eventually appreciate this. She'll see that if I'm willing to do something this big for a stranger, she'll know I'd do literally anything for her and the girls. She'll come around, warm up to it, maybe even admire it in time.*

Vilda sent word. Surgery date: September 15, 2021.

September 13 was hard. Rachel had been in Idaho visiting family, so

I had the kids alone. I woke early and spent the morning getting the girls ready for school. Grace, now ten, was in fourth grade, and Georgie, soon to be seven, was in first grade. It was school-picture day, so I worked extra hard on the hair part, knowing that should I fail my picture-prep mission, there would be evidence (and consequences).

I got them to school and said goodbye. Rachel and I decided not to tell them about the transplant surgery. We thought it would be best to explain after all was clear postsurgery. Daddy was going on a "work trip."

Rachel got back from Idaho to the Colorado Springs airport just ahead of my departure from the same airport. I met her there, on a bench in front of the terminal on a sunny day, flowers in hand. Bouquet notwithstanding, the conversation soured.

"Hi," I greeted her the best I could. Her body language was negative.

"Hi," she responded flatly. Her body language somehow doubled the negativity in the space of a single word.

"I don't want you to do this," she said. "You haven't listened to me at all; you haven't listened to a word I've said. You've only thought about yourself. Not us."

She brought up the risk of death again. What might happen to the family. She knew I had been concerned enough to make arrangements just in case. It may have been small, but the risk was there, and she wasn't the only one to bring up this or other risks. A friend had also asked, "Why are you risking your marriage for a stranger?"

Sitting next to Rachel on that bench, I thought about that question, because it seemed like that was exactly what was happening. I didn't really know what to say, so I leaned on the numbers. "You know that the risk is lower than when you gave birth to either of the girls, and we never worried about that at all," I said.

"The girls are *our daughters*. This is someone we don't even know!"

I didn't have a response. Not a good one. And like most arguments between couples, the words just exposed the icy tip, with a far larger mass of iceberg beneath and between us. I left worried, very worried, about us and whether there would be an "us" in the near future. At the same time I felt like I had done everything to make this work; I was wide open to talk and change. But if it wasn't going to be enough, then it just wasn't enough. I didn't know whether or not our marriage would hold, but I was certain that I could save a life, maybe several, and I so very badly wanted to.

So I acted on that certainty and hoped for the best with everything else.

Newly sick to my stomach, I boarded the plane.

The next morning at Walter Reed, I saw Vilda for my pre-surgery Covid test. I told her I was looking forward to checking in the next day.

"Matt, what do you mean? You need to check into the hospital tonight. Didn't you know?" Vilda scolded me.

I must've missed something. Because the girls were in school, Rachel had to stay at home, and my mom offered to be my postsurgery chaperone. I then rushed to arrange for Mom to get to Walter Reed on her own while I was in surgery.

Way back in grade school I drew my mom as a dove, which is accurate but maybe incomplete because it misses just how tough she is. Once on a vacation in Scotland, she fell, felt a shock of pain in her midsection, and kept on with the trip—only to find out weeks later at home that she'd broken a rib.

After college, where she was an all-sport cheerleader at the University of Minnesota, Mom pivoted into elementary special education, and she absolutely loved being a teacher, an attitude she carried home with her every night.

When I had a project due in early grade school, I left my diorama-and-description assignment until the last minute. It was due on a Monday, and I hadn't started by late Friday. When I confessed my crime of lateness to her, and I asked if she might write a note to my teacher to move the due date later, she refused, canceled all weekend fun, and made me work every waking minute of the weekend until it was done.

It was a sweatshop, elementary school style. Scissors and glue until my fingers and nose couldn't take it anymore. I don't recall how I did gradewise (probably not well), but I remember, to this day, the real lesson my mom stapled onto my soul: Deadlines matter. They're promises in calendar form, and we keep our promises, no matter the cost.

That afternoon, after making arrangements for Mom, I had a last glass of red wine to say goodbye to my left kidney in the hotel restaurant. It felt like I'd indirectly shared a long-distance drink with my recipient, like a sip might stay in the kidney long enough to make it to the other side.

I left at 5:15 PM for the hospital, and on arrival, changed into a hypercool empty-backed gown. I cleaned my midsection and groin with paper-towel-sized surgical wipes. They gave me yellow booties with little rubber pads on the bottoms and slapped a yellow bracelet on my wrist that read, in big black letters, "FALL RISK."

"Is this just for me?" I asked the nurse. "Do I look particularly wobbly?"

"Everyone, man. Not just you," came his flat response.

At 3 AM, the nurse woke me and wheeled me down for surgery. It had to be so early because my recipient was on the West Coast. My kidney was to board a plane to Seattle and be there in time for the recipient's procedure. *At least part of me made it to first class*, I thought, as the nurse parked my bed alongside a wall in a partially darkened hallway, where I met two nice anesthesiologists.

We talked, and as everything faded to black, I remembered a moment from Iraq in 2003 like a bad dream . . .

I had fired every bullet and it wasn't enough.

I was a cocky twenty-three-year-old lieutenant, fresh from West Point, defending our cavalry squadron's position west of Baghdad, in Fallujah, on a black night in May 2003. My mission: guard our squadron's base camp, filled with hundreds and hundreds of soldiers asleep a half mile to my rear. I sat atop a Bradley Fire Support Team vehicle, an armored vehicle a little smaller than a tank, overlooking the field below. In the distance were several walled-off housing compounds, with a road running in front of them. I scanned the area with my night-vision goggles. A young soldier—Private First Class Jones[7]—sat beneath me in the vehicle, on a break from looking out into the Iraqi night.

Crack! Crack! Crack!

Tracer fire flamed the sky, and the bright light forced me to pull off my goggles. I grabbed my rifle, fired back, then yelled, "Jones, get up here! Get up here *now*!"

No response.

Tracer bullets continued to light up the sky like bolts of Halloween glow sticks that visually confirm the firer's on target; if the man-made lightning bolt goes wide right, then you pull left, etc. They're usually fitted into an ammunition clip every five or six regular bullets.

"Shit!" I yelled as a bullet hit the dirt to my right. Then, directed down below, "Jones, where the *fuck* are you?"

No response.

I put down my M4 rifle, reached for the radio, and called in to the headquarters' tactical operations center. We were trained to give the simplest contact report possible using "SALT," an acronym for the enemy's size, activity, location, and time.

---

7 A pseudonym.

It was so dark, but based on what I could see, I shouted, "Sabre X-ray, this is Fox Redleg—contact, contact, contact—squad-size element; firing small arms at my position; four hundred meters to my twelve o'clock; time *now*. Over!"

The response: "Fox Redleg, this is Sabre X-ray, read you lima charlie.[8] Sending QRF. Stand by."

While more than a little pissed off at how calm the radio guy was as bullets struck around me, I thought, *Good, they're sending the quick reaction force. Cavalry's coming. But where's Jones?*

"Jones!"

No response.

I fired more. I was atop a vehicle with an absolute beast of a main gun that could put out 25 millimeter rounds (compared to my rifle's puny 5.56 millimeter rounds). If Jones was with me, we could answer with that main gun. Without him I was stuck with my rifle, because I needed to watch and stay on the radio to keep headquarters informed on the firefight.

But there was a problem. Normally a soldier's basic load was seven magazines, each containing thirty rounds, for a total of 210 bullets. I had one magazine in my rifle when the attack started, and then four more strapped to my vest. The other two were stashed in the Bradley below, in my rucksack, far out of reach.

So I fired what I had. First magazine . . . emptied with a *click*. Reload.

Then another . . . *click*. Next mag.

Then another. Then another. I was down to my last one. I slowed my fire for an eternity—that lasted a few dozen seconds.

Then, finally—*click*. I was out.

Black on ammo, I went Winchester—out of ammunition, which any soldier will tell you is the worst moment there is because you're helpless.

---

8 "Loud and clear."

Vulnerable. Completely vulnerable. You've gone from an asset to a liability, and I knew it was only minutes until *they* knew I was out.

The tracers kept on and a bullet pinged off the Bradley, so sharp it felt like the sound alone might slice skin. That's when I felt the most sickening emptiness I had ever felt in my life. I did everything I could with what I had, and it was all going to end right there, right then.

I looked out at the dark sky and thought, *I'm done. This is it.*

When the last bullet ran out, I didn't pray; I panicked. I pulled my right hand off the now-useless trigger and picked up the radio one last time and opened my mouth to get an update on the team coming to help. And that's when I saw them to the left. Humvee lights. They fired and quickly drove off the attack.

Just like that, it was over.

That night, I was too shaken to sleep. I later learned Jones had run down the hill and across the half mile back to camp, afraid to fight back. In the chaos and the overwhelm after it all, I never found the QRF team that turned back the attack.

They saved my life, and I didn't even know their names.

That night I learned how fragile life is. I learned how much I rely on others, even strangers. And I learned how it feels to receive true grace when you need it the most.

Then, eighteen years later, I got to be the cavalry. I got to pay it forward.

I woke up groggy in the ICU, about 8 AM, just as Vilda briefed me I would. I had trouble opening my eyes for a couple hours because I was so sleepy from the surgery meds still in my system. But Mom was there, and I was with-it enough by 10 AM to call Rachel and tell her I was OK, just as she dropped the kids off at school back home in Colorado.

When I could manage, I pushed the tubes aside and pulled my gown across my body to see my stomach. The nurses narrated to me what happened.

One surgeon had made four tiny incisions in a vertical pattern on my abdomen's left side. That was for tools and a camera to enable the surgeon to do the work with robotic arms and a computer monitor and joystick. The advantage of this procedure was that no human hands went inside my abdomen, which speeds recovery. When they had separated the kidney, the surgeon made about a pointer-finger-length incision, horizontal, below my navel, just big enough to pop the kidney out when the work was done. My kidney was packed in ice and taken to the airport. In about three hours, my robot-assisted, laparoscopic nephrectomy was complete.

I was down to one kidney.[9]

The next few days passed in a haze.

The doctors told me that my recipient successfully received the kidney and was to be discharged the same day as me. After I showed them I could go the bathroom (both ways), I was released.

Mom and I checked into our hotel rooms near the National Mall in Washington where we stayed for six days after the surgery, just long enough to get a post-op checkup and be cleared for a flight home. Our schedule was simple. We would get up, have breakfast, walk to a museum or two or three every day.

9 The transplant team took a picture of my kidney just after removal, a gross photographic souvenir that was weirdly reassuring. (How else would I know what they'd taken out?) I've also since learned that it's common for donors to do a before/after selfie, something I skipped. I'm a flip phone guy, not much into selfies, and to me at the time this was all just a medical procedure, not such a big deal, a one-off and then back to normal life. (Boy, was I wrong.)

My midsection was sore. The hardest part was the descent into bed and then the ascent up from bed. I developed a sketchy side-roll technique that got the job done, but just barely, and even I would acknowledge it was super risky and super dumb.

I also learned about guts and gravity. I have always been a side sleeper. That first night I turned onto my side, and when I did, I audibly heard my guts move inside my body.

Freaked out, I sat up and turned the lights on.

What was that? Some kind of slimy mouse in the bed? I freaked out, then thought again.

Of course! The empty space!

I figured what was left in there jockeyed for new positions inside my body. The remaining organs filled in the extra space ("Nature abhors a vacuum," said some science professor at some point in my life, and this had to be the grossest vacuum ever). Thankfully it only lasted another couple nights. After that, everything settled.

But as gross as that was, it wasn't as disgusting as my behavior at dinner that Sunday night, September 19, when I proved that giving away a kidney doesn't mean anyone surgically removed my asshole.

I took Mom to dinner at Supra, a Georgian (former Soviet, not Atlanta) restaurant in Washington. I really wanted to eat something good, really good, and this was it. Conversation turned to my younger years, specifically high school. There had been a moment on my high school hockey team when our coach had warned us not to break the rules on chewing tobacco.[10]

Our team had a bad loss, and postgame, as I walked onto the team bus, there were a couple players dipping in the open. As a team captain,

---

10 Which, years later, having served in the Army as long as I had, chew and dip were regular features at unit meetings. No big deal. However, in high school hockey, it was a very big deal.

it was my place to tell them to spit it out (if they were caught, the entire team would face consequences). The two guys essentially told me to fuck off, to mind my own business.

When the bus got back, I told the coaches what had happened, and the two players were later suspended for a couple weeks. From then on I was ostracized and worse by a certain group of players and parents. Some weirdo parent even wrote an awful, anonymous letter and dropped it in our home's mailbox. One of the suspended guys tried to goad me into a fight while I walked with my girlfriend. It was rough. My parents disagreed with my decision to report the two guys. Then, and since, I thought it was the hard but right thing to do.

During dinner at Supra, I deliberately brought it up with Mom. With a whiff of arrogance, I told her I still thought she and Dad were wrong.

Here my mom was, taking time out of her retirement and her life to help me while on the mend, and I raised a serious friction point from over two decades ago. It was stupid. It was wrong. It was petty. She threatened to walk from dinner. (She should have.) We finished in silence.

Here I was, days—heck, hours—after the kindest act of generosity I had ever participated in—and I baited my own mom into a ridiculous argument. What a schmuck.

People assume that kidney donors are kind, angelic, even saintly. I'm clearly not.

After I apologized to Mom, we made up, and the next day we parted ways at the airport. I sat in Reagan National passing time. I rummaged through the bag of painkilling meds the hospital gave me. Under the pile of plastic pill tubes, I found and opened the manila envelope that held the discharge paperwork. I scanned, and halfway down the page read recovery instructions that gave me pause and made me wonder if the doctors were messing with me. It said:

"You can march in place, no running or sit-ups for six months."

Are they serious? Is this for real?

ACTION THIS DAY

Cut everything away, and this chapter demonstrates that an imperfect, flawed person can do something good for another person.

Are you imperfect? Are you flawed?

I thought so. I mean, we all are in some way, right?

So there's no excuse. You don't have to rip out an organ and give it to someone you bump into on the bus. But just because you can't be everything for everybody doesn't mean you can't do something for someone.

Start today. Now. Just one kind act. Try it. I dare you.

Who knows, it may change your life.

It did mine. You'll see.

Chapter Two

FORTUNE FAVORS THE BOLD

This one pure, bold act gave me purpose, direction, clarity, focus. Like I knew who I was and what I was meant to do.

October 3, 2021
Manitou Springs, Colorado

Two weeks after my surgery, Grace had a cross-country race. It was on two grassy rugby fields side by side that the organization—called the Landsharks—had the kids run two laps around. We cheered Grace on as she ran wearing her yellow shirt with a giant two-legged shark logo on the front. It was the kind of race that had no designated spectator area and no barriers, so what typically happened was some parents would get excited and rush off across the field to jog alongside and cheer in closer proximity to their running kiddos.

Georgie jogged off to see Grace. I followed across the field and noticed that at her speed, Georgie wouldn't intercept Grace on the course. She needed a boost. Without thinking, I picked Georgie up, pulled her onto my back, and kept on at a light jog toward Grace.

By then Rachel had gotten up and chased after us. The moment she got close to me—and my new Georgie backpack—Rachel half yelled over the cheering parents, "What are you doing! You just had surgery!"

What *was* I doing? Just as important—*how* was I doing?

My body felt good. I still had what looked like the equivalent of a pointer finger surgically implanted beneath the incision site, just below my navel, the spot where they'd cut through the abdominal wall. But I was healing. I saw progress. My body was adjusting to the new operating system. The doctors warned me I'd feel fatigued now and again, and I did notice I had to get to bed a little earlier, that I was more tired than usual later in the day. But that symptom trailed off after about a month. Around then, my first blood test showed I was back to normal, healthy kidney function range.

I gave myself some time to heal, then started pushing myself, walking more and more. I dedicated myself to rising early and walking with the same drive I would to train for a marathon. More than power walks, these turbo walks went up and down the main drag in Manitou. The better I felt the more I walked. The more I walked the better I felt. I'd go so early it was just me and the street-sweeper guy. Because it was now October, my pre-work walks were all in the morning darkness.

It wasn't just dark outside; I felt the dark inside my head and inside my marriage. It got even worse as I inched closer and closer to the end of my Army career, a career that had spanned my entire adult life. I was at a crossroads, personally and professionally. The kidney donation felt like a reason to pause and focus on the coming fork in the road. At that point, while my mind didn't know which way to go, at least my body was still moving forward.

It was the one spark of light in the dark. On October 12, just under a month after surgery, I ran for the first time. I did about 2.5 miles slow, then walked 1.5 miles, then two more miles jogging. It felt super.

Getting back to the run meant something to me. I'd been a runner since I returned from my second tour in Iraq in 2006. I'd picked up a copy of Dean Karnazes's bestselling book *Ultramarathon Man,* and I was hooked. Reading it inspired me to start finding my way through marathons and beyond. I became good enough to run a 2:38 personal best (just over six minutes per mile for 26.2 miles) at the Marine Corps Marathon in 2009, and, eventually, I got off the pavement to find a passion for trail running. The trails led me to the TransRockies Run, a six-day, 120-mile stage race in Colorado with 20,000 feet of climbing and an average of over 10,000 feet elevation across the week. The stages are about twenty miles per day, and while the race requires some mandatory gear for inclement weather, it is fully supported, meaning the race provides food and care, even including a daily shower. Initially, after surgery, getting back to being able to run the TransRockies was my physical goal.

But it wasn't the only thing on my mind. While I felt a little overwhelmed with life generally, with my marriage and career, I did have one other big, bright spot. The radical generosity of donation gave me this psychological boost—a big, burning holy fire inside powered by a river of rocket fuel—and I wanted to share it. I had this recurring thought running laps in my head, *Someone's alive because of me!* I wanted more people to know how this felt—to know that you can donate a kidney, save a life, and go on to live a healthy, full life of your own.

I wrote about it. I wrote about my kidney donation in an essay for *The Los Angeles Times* on October 17, 2021. A guy named Ned Brooks, another kidney donor and founder of the National Kidney Donation Organization, read the essay and reached out. In turn, he put me in touch with the National Kidney Registry (NKR), the organization that had set up my donation chain.

On Tuesday, October 26, I went to marriage counseling with Rachel in the early afternoon. It did not go well. In fact, it went the opposite of well. She told me she wasn't sure if she had ever loved me. As in *ever.* It felt like part of me broke in that room. Everything went numb.

After we walked out of the blocky concrete building and parted ways, I didn't want to do anything. But I had promised to listen in to a conference call with the NKR about their athletic programs. Right in the lot, among rows of neatly parked cars, I listened in on my phone as a staff member mentioned, offhand, that they'd recently commissioned a poll that found that 75 percent of Americans had the misperception that kidney donation degrades the donor physically. Feeling in my bones how wrongheaded that was, even so close after my own donation, I found that figure appalling. I also heard NKR's CEO, Garet Hil, say he was interested to hear ideas that might help turn this number around, so that more people would feel inclined to donate without undue concern for future health. I left the call wondering what I could do to shatter that misperception. I thought: *What if I tried to run more than I could before?* My background at the TransRockies Run sent me looking for related but greater challenges—and I found one.

Three days after the conference call, on Friday, October 29, I sent Hil an email, which read, in part:

> There's a big, tough set of trail races called the 4 Deserts series—each is 155 miles over 7 days in brutal conditions (self-supported, carry everything, except water and tent). Doing 4 in a calendar year is called a "slam," and only 78 have completed it since 2008.
>
> It's in the Namib/Namibia (early May), Gobi/Mongolia, (late June), Atacama/Chile (late September), and Antarctica/the "White Desert" (late November).
>
> You can see where I'm going . . .
>
> Honestly, this would be an enormous undertaking. Just the running itself—28 days of near-marathon distances over a few months in deserts

> carrying 20+ pounds of gear. (As much as I like running, just typing that's a little ridiculous.) And the potential for bad weather—this past year at the Marathon des Sables (another Sahara race) the temps got to over 130 degrees F—makes this riskier.
>
> I haven't run any of this by my wife (which is usually where I get into trouble, especially if it means missing Thanksgiving), so I'd still put this in the wild idea category. And taking that much work off would be tough, but likely doable.
>
> Your thoughts? Something NKR might consider backing?

Hil wrote back immediately: "I like the idea and we would consider backing it."

By early December, NKR green-lit the idea. We called it "1K4D," shorthand for "one kidney, four deserts." I started blogging on NKR's website to show what could be possible in order to nudge others toward donation.

I wasn't even seven weeks postsurgery, and I had just pledged to run 1,000 kilometers, wearing a pack, across some of the harshest terrain on Earth. I'd only ever raced 120 fully supported miles over six days in one year; this was to be 620 self-supported miles over twenty-four days on four continents. Far more than I'd ever done when I had two kidneys.

Maybe I was running away from something. Maybe I was running to something. But I knew I just needed to run.

That moment's intensity brought to mind the time I had an Army assignment a decade earlier in New Zealand. Just north of Wellington was a military base where part of the Royal New Zealand Infantry Regiment was stationed. There I saw a sign describing one of the unit's historical mottos: "Virtutis Fortuna Comes" (*fortune is the companion of virtue*). This is a differently worded version of a 2,000-year-old Latin proverb, used once in *The Aeneid* by Virgil: *fortune favors the bold*. Military units around the world have used *fortune favors the bold* to signify the power of decisiveness. Choice and violence of action can have a big impact on outcome.

To ask for 1K4D was to double down, to lean even further into the decision to donate in the first place. Correspondingly, the stakes went up. Double the risk, and maybe double the reward if I could inspire more donors.

This one pure, bold act gave me purpose, direction, clarity, focus. Like I knew who I was and what I was meant to do. Nothing in my life felt like it was really working, and then I had done something that actually worked by donating, and I didn't want that feeling to stop. Running advocacy might show others they have an extra kidney to give and that some have none, the medical equivalent of breaking a bread loaf in half to share with someone who's starving. I could keep paying it forward through running.

I felt fortune smile on me over the next few months.

Training spiked instantly. I worked with a coach—Jason Koop of Carmichael Training Systems, one of the best in ultrarunning.

I ran 204 miles in December 2021 and ramped up to 408 miles in March 2022. Double. From 50 miles per week to over 100 miles per week. That's nuts.

Even nuttier was that I worked a full-time job as an active-duty Army officer. I did all those miles in the dark before the workday. I would run an early-morning marathon, then work a day that felt like another marathon. I easily consumed twice the caffeine a human should. Shower, sleep, repeat.

I also registered for all four races with RacingThePlanet. They bombarded me with emails. One salvo with medical requirements, then another with travel information. And that was just one race. (Multiply that times four for all the events.) The Namib Race was first up and fast approaching, so I had to book travel before I even had formal approval from the military to participate (which would later become the rowdiest goat rodeo ever).

But by far the most demanding, troubling, and nerve-wracking was the mandatory equipment list. Failure to meet the requirements meant I wouldn't be allowed to race. The packing list included thirty-seven items, in addition to guidance for drop bags and optional equipment. I obsessed over that list—particularly my pack, my shoes (how to keep sand out), and hydration in the desert.

Enter John Bezou, a tall, dark-haired New Orleans native. If you squinted, you'd see a rougher, more athletic version of Harry Connick Jr. Nearly all the other Grand Slammers were from faraway places like Germany and Japan, but, remarkably, John was from one zip code over in Colorado Springs.

When I registered, someone at RacingThePlanet noticed my address was very near John's. They put us in contact, and we met at a local brewery for a drink. We had a lot in common. John had recently retired after an Army career. His last assignment was as director of the human performance optimization program at an infantry division, with strength coaches, dieticians, athletic trainers, and performance psychology professionals on speed dial.

I skipped all but the barest pleasantries, just went straight to the dumb-new-guy questions. "Tell me how I should pack, man." No bush beating for me.

"I was all set to do the Grand Slam in 2020," John explained in the middle of a list of packing tips, "but then Covid canceled everything. So I've just been waiting and learning everything I can these past couple years about how to do these races."

John talked about his transition to endurance coaching, a natural move after having worked with soldier-athletes. He named his company Hypoxia Performance, after the medical term for a lack of oxygen supply at the tissue level. John explained the name's backstory.

"I was new to Colorado Springs," he said, "and a buddy took me on a hike up Pikes Peak, over fourteen thousand feet, and when we got up out above the tree line I was staggering around. My buddy called me the 'Hypoxia Kid,' and it stuck, and after a while I just liked the way it sounded."

"Hey man, every superhero has an origin story—even the Hypoxia Kid!" I said. "Now tell me how to eat at races like this." This was my other great concern. The race required 14,000 calories for the week. You can carry more if you want to, but the trade-off is the additional weight.

I had no idea how or what to pack. I had done many races before and knew what my stomach would tolerate pre-race and in race, but I had never had to pack for an entire week. Trying to pack all the calories I'd consume during that time and loading them all in a backpack to carry around while running a marathon every day—yikes.

John pointed out that nuts and olive oil are calorie dense, nearly two hundred calories per ounce, and that both could be useful additions. Not one for nuts, I got some small individual-sized olive oil packets and immediately threw them in my bag.

"What about hydration? Electrolytes?" I asked, and continued, "You know my kidney thing."

John said, "DripDrop, it's the best; I highly recommend it. It's what we handed out to everyone when I was working. Try some." He just happened to have a couple packets on him.

I would later take forty-eight packets of DripDrop to the Namib, a small slice of the 19,945 calories I would carry in my pack.

What luck it was to meet John. He was a coach—an actual running coach—so he knew how to explain things for someone like me.

I had a guy—who rapidly became a close friend—who'd been preparing for this race for years and who could now help me prepare. What luck.

Then I ran eighty-three total miles on March 11, 12, and 13—more than I had ever run in three days in my life. My previous three-day high was somewhere in the sixty-mile range. I beat that by one-third. In this way, One-Kidney Matt became 133 percent of Two-Kidney Matt. I was upgraded.

I wondered: *What if we're stronger, better, more with one less kidney?*

Recall that when I was discharged from the hospital, the nurse handed me a piece of paper that directed me, in no uncertain terms, not to run for six months. Just to put an exclamation point on it, I highlighted the restricted activity paragraph, and then underlined the key part of the sentence that read: "You can march in place, no running or sit-ups for 6 months."

If I had followed that advice, I wouldn't have run until March 15, 2022. Not one stride.

I didn't follow that advice.

Why should I have?[11]

Of course, there are trade-offs to our physical selves, but what if emotional and psychological health is so boosted after a kidney donation that we are more than what we were before?

I meant that. I recognized I was only a data point of one. A single anecdote. A one-off. A story. But my experience was just that—someone whose life had been boosted by kidney donation.

That's what 1K4D—the entire experiment—seemed to be about. I was eager to test the hypothesis: *Can you be more with less? Can your life get bigger when you give up something small for someone else? Could you be a better athlete on a single kidney?*

---

11 Okay, okay, there is a slight hernia risk.

Am I more than I was before?
The Namib was where I found my answer. It wasn't what I expected.

ACTION THIS DAY

There is power in decision. In seeing and setting a course, notwithstanding all the natural unknowns that float out there in front of us like clouds in the sky. But for some risks, numbers don't matter. Sometimes you go even if you don't know. Maybe the best time to think big is when you feel small.

When I think about risky decisions, I always come back to a story I heard when I was a cadet (I jotted down the author as Leslie D. Weatherhead, though I can't confirm its precise origin). The story's likely legend, but that doesn't diminish its power:

> When a soldier was injured and could not get back to safety, his buddy went out to get him, against his officer's orders. He returned mortally wounded, and his friend, whom he had carried back, was dead.
>
> The officer was angry. "I told you not to go," he said. "Now I've lost both of you. It wasn't worth it."
>
> The dying man replied, "But it was, sir, because when I got to him, he said, 'Jim, I knew you'd come.'"

Of course, we should account for risks as best we can. But in the end, we often find that it's not about the numbers—it's about what the risk means to you.

It's usually as simple as *How bad do you want it*? Or even *Is this worth dying for?*

If the answers are "not so bad" and "no," then walk away. Keep your powder dry for next time.

If the answers are "really bad" and "yes," then fight. Keep going, no matter how poor the odds.

In the end, numbers can't give you the meaning you need.

Only you can.

Chapter Three

MURPHY'S LAW

Murphy didn't want me on that start line.

March 17, 2022
Manitou Springs, Colorado

It wasn't even 7 AM and my hands were blue like Smurf mitts.

My legs shuffled unsteadily as I returned home from my early-morning training run. I had to be at work in an hour. It's a rough start to Saint Patrick's Day when you look drunk a dozen hours ahead of everybody else.

"Murphy's gonna get you," a senior sergeant used to tell me, an entirely appropriate memory for my start to St. Paddy's Day. He'd needle me about being the "fifty-pound brain" guy—meaning I had been taught too much book-smart stuff and not enough real-life stuff.

Murphy's Law—the idea that anything that can go wrong will go wrong (and at the worst time)—is credited to Edward Murphy, a 1940 West Point graduate, who came up with the idea during rocket tests (and associated mishaps).

For the record, Murph got me that day.

Right after my eighty-three-mile moment I got a little cocky. Okay, not a little. Big cocky. Ten-feet-tall cocky.

I figured I had this. Easy. No sweat. I figured, *What was another twenty-two-mile training run?*

Boy was I wrong. First there was the springtime-in-Colorado weather. Sleet and wet snow, the kind that thickens and sticks to you like syrup. Then there was the salt. Or, I should say, my lack of salt. I didn't take any electrolytes.

Strike three was how I dressed. I had been overdressing to force sweat and prepare for the desert environment. But this morning I'd taken it to new heights. I wore an extra jacket that the wet weather soaked, and it then chilled me to my marrow.

The result was predictable.

I hit the midpoint right on mark and felt good. I had left the house at 4 AM and was bang on for the turnaround at 5:20 AM. But then I started to bleed out strength. I got weaker and weaker. My pace drifted down. I made it to mile seventeen, with five miles to go to get home, and I was in a death shuffle.

I felt this combination of sick and weak and confused and feeble and broke and ashamed and mad and tunnel-visioned. I couldn't see straight. The edges of the frame got fuzzy. It's something I know from experience, unfortunately.

I trudged through mile seventeen, then eighteen, then nineteen, and into mile twenty.

When I got to the midpoint of the twentieth mile, I gave in and walked. I stumbled in the house, barely made it up the stairs to the bathroom. Rachel followed me up.

"Are you okay? You need anything?" she asked.

"I'm . . . okay," I responded slowly, as if I was attempting the world's raspiest, worst Christian Bale–Batman impression.

She was worried. She had good reason, even beyond my Saint Patrick's Day massacre.

A few days before, I had been in the living room watching a

documentary about the 4 Deserts race series called *Desert Runners*. It covered the 2010 class of Grand Slammers and featured four amateur runners from around the world.

Midway through the documentary, during a stage in the Gobi Desert, the temperature rose sharply over the course of the day. An American runner in his early thirties, Nick Kruse, collapsed a mile from the stage's finish and had to be evacuated off course slumped over a camel. The race announced that he later died.

Of all the moments, this was the scene on screen when Rachel walked in the living room. She looked on in horror at the television and said, "Are you serious? Are you really going to do *this*?"

Her question came a week after a world-renowned kidney doctor, having heard that I'd gotten a doctor's permission to race, asked somewhat angrily, "What nephrologist cleared you to do this race? Don't you know what kind of damage you might do to your remaining kidney?"

I didn't ignore his concern outright. I just felt in my heart and gut that this was the right thing to do, that I was an experienced runner, and that I had worked diligently to prepare and reduce risk wherever I could. Even if I didn't have solid answers to satisfy every sharp question, I had faith it would all work out. Faith in part due to my training. I'd run three three-day stretches of 71 miles, 77 miles, and 83 miles. In total, for the five months leading up to the Namib Race from December 2021 through April 2022, I ran 114 workouts spanning 188 hours and covering 1,352 miles. If my body was going to fail on me, it should've happened during training.

But still, that faith was tested. Murphy was with me every step of the way to Namibia. My old sergeant would've loved it.

Murphy didn't want me on that start line.

It began with the torturous process of getting military approval for travel to Namibia. As an active-duty Army lieutenant colonel, not only did I have to get permission from my boss to go, but I also had to go through three other separate bureaucratic processes, including two separate military commands on two different continents and then the US State Department. The checklist included eleven vaccinations, a section where I had to pinpoint five different locations I would go in case of a terrorist attack, and I had to agree to email a military headquarters every single day while racing to provide proof of life.

I sliced through red tape with both arms swinging machetes, but I still didn't get final approval until the day before departure.

I woke excruciatingly early, at 2 AM, at home on April 26. Because Namibia is eight hours ahead of Colorado, I got up so early to start my time shift, but also because I had some last-minute packing to do.

I got out my thirty-seven mandatory race items once more to confirm all was okay. I divided my gear into absolutely must-have items that I would carry with me onto the plane and then the items in my checked bag that could be replaced if the airline misplaced anything.

We loaded up the car with my bags, the kids, and Grace's fourth-grade class project.[12] By 7:30 AM I sat in the small Colorado Springs airport waiting for my flight to Denver. My itinerary had me flying from Denver on to two major airports before a final flight to Walvis Bay, on the Namibian coast near our linkup point in the city of Swakopmund on April 28.

When I landed in Denver, I turned my phone on to see a text message from the airline:

> We're sorry to let you know we've cancelled your flight from Newark to Johannesburg because of airport conditions preventing your departure.

---

12 A salt-dough physical map of Colorado, each region painted for elevation differences.

Not only was that flight canceled, but the next day I had another flight to Africa canceled, making two consecutive days with intercontinental flight cancellations. It took another forty-eight hours of travel and over 10,000 air miles before I finally made it. My flight touched down in Windhoek, Namibia, a little after 8 AM on April 28.

The huge quantity of squashed bugs that lined the tarmac from the plane to the terminal gave me my first impression of Namibia. Some appeared to be steroid-injected crickets, others giganto beetles, even some mongo locusts. I tried to keep my feet from the goo as I entered the terminal.

After showing my vaccination status and passport, I stepped through a customs check line into the terminal where I instantly saw the shuttle service. A man named Vernon told me that due to my late flight changes, I wouldn't go on the shuttle straight from Windhoek to Swakopmund but instead by taxi to the nearby Roof of Africa hotel, connect with others from the race, and then proceed to Swakopmund later that afternoon.

A driver collected me and Ivan—a bald, sinewy Dane in his sixties—and his partner of many years, Janka, an outgoing, kind, German life coach with a loud voice filled with warmth.

As we climbed into the taxi, I looked down at my body's first physical casualty of the trip—my ankles, which had disappeared. My legs now extended several inches south, white fleshy fat extending over where my ankle joints once were. Gross.

I was gross too. When we got to the Roof of Africa I went into the bathroom and evaluated myself. Everything was greasy. My hair looked like I'd dunked it in motor oil.

As gross as I felt, lunch with Ivan and Janka was amazing. I hadn't talked to anyone outside of high-stakes interactions with airline ticket agents in days. They told me about an ultrarace Ivan had done in Costa Rica the year before where it rained for hours every day. One stretch was supposed to be along a low-level river, but it had flooded, so he had to swim with his pack and was worried for his life. Janka had gone as a volunteer and set up and took down soggy tents all week. Though they chuckled about it now, and did enjoy the trip, both were overjoyed to be at a desert race because the one thing they could count on was no rain.

After lunch, our shuttle driver showed at about the same time as Julita from Poland walked in. A tall gym teacher with bright blonde hair and a bright smile to match, she was a former Polish *Ninja Warrior* contestant.

We threw our bags in the trailer hitched to the back of the little bus. The driver pointed us west for the five-hour drive to Swakopmund, located on the coast.

We pulled into Swakopmund close to 6 PM. We all checked into our hotel, a century-old converted train station built by German colonists. It had a pale-yellow exterior with white trim and a courtyard that surrounded an oasis-like pool. After a speedy shower and change of clothes, I met Julita near the front desk, and we hopped a ride to the Swakopmund Plaza Hotel, where we could take our pre-race Covid tests.

On arrival, Julita and I chatted with other runners, all of us trying to avoid thinking the unthinkable. Anyone who tested positive wouldn't be permitted to race. We would learn the results the next day by noon.

There we also met the race director, Sam Fanshawe, a British woman who I'd been in contact with via email for months. After a few welcome remarks, Sam turned things over to the testers.

When my turn came to get swabbed, my tester, wearing full hazmat suit and goggles, shoved the gargantuan Q-tip so deep in my cranium the backs of my eyes felt cotton. I squirmed, and as soon as it cleared my nostril, I leapt and sprinted to the room's corner to explode with a sneeze heard round the room.

Julita laughed and proceeded to sit and take the swab without so much as a sniffle.

We walked back to the hotel, exhausted, as the sun set.

The next morning I finally bumped into John Bezou. He was excited to see me. I'd been out of contact on the long travel in, and he wasn't sure I'd made the trip. John was with Mike, a veterinarian from Miami. Mike was a little stockier than John, with big eyes that made him look perpetually surprised. Mike had already done five of these events, and John mentioned Mike knew his stuff.

John came by my room and looked down at my gear strewn about the floor. He pointed at the freeze-dried meals still in their original packaging.

"You need help with those? I've got extra bags for those."

"I left them in the original packaging to get through the flights," I responded. "Thought it might be good to leave for the race inspection."

"Don't worry about that," John said. "They'll trust you have the calories you tell them is in each."

I showed John the spreadsheet with my calories listed out.

"Yeah, you'll be fine, just show them that."

John told me he had about 18,000 calories, and as I was just shy of 20,000, it felt good to know I was close to his number. He then got out some small ziplock bags and helped me fit my powdery dehydrated meals into them. I wrote the meal name on each bag with a black marker, as well as the calorie and water amount to add for rehydration.

With this operation ongoing, Mike walked back in and laughed weirdly. He muttered and looked right at me, "What is with these people? Haven't you seen all the videos I've posted on social media?"

I looked back and said, "No, I haven't . . . what videos?"

He seemed annoyed, mentioned needing to be somewhere, and walked out.

John explained Mike had been doing a lot of videos about race packing on social media. Because he was so experienced, he could be opinionated about how to pack.

Great, I thought, *now I know for sure I don't know what I'm doing.*

One more sleep.

Then the desert.

ACTION THIS DAY

A close corollary to Murphy's Law is that pain is provided and pleasure is permitted. We will always find larger quantities of difficulty than comfort, more hardship than fun. Malady comes by default, smiles take effort.

Never forget that no matter what we do, Murphy will get us all. Maybe the best we can do is draw Murphy out. Ambush him. Rehearse, rehearse, rehearse until he's out in the open, we see what Murphy throws at us, and thereby maximize our preparedness.

That's what I did.

As I left for Namibia, I found myself pondering the thought, attributed to Lao Tzu: "The journey of 1,000 miles begins with a single step."

It's not exactly true. I should know. I went on a journey of 1,000 kilometers.

When I got to the starting line, there was, of course, that literal first step.

But it took a lot more than that—a whole lot more—to make the journey possible.

There was the initial idea, the pitch, and then support from the National Kidney Registry. And then lining up a coach, gathering the gear, planning the travel, and getting the okay from work to be away for so long.

Then the training: 1,352 miles.

I did just about everything I could to draw Murphy out.

My journey of 1,000 kilometers began with over 1,300 miles run.

Was it enough?

Chapter Four

NO PLAN SURVIVES CONTACT

RACE ACROSS THE OLDEST DESERT—THE NAMIB

The trouble was, when you felt good there, you knew it couldn't last.

April 29, 2022
Swakopmund, Namibia

They look magic, I thought.

On the hour-long bus ride from our Swakopmund hotel to the first camp we saw massive, multistory dunes along the road on one side and the ocean on the other. Late in the afternoon the bus turned off the coastal road at a salt factory with enormous white pyramids. They looked like giant piles of salt in the distance.

As we drove, I read the race guide and realized the people on this bus were the hardest of hard asses. Titanium hard. Vibranium hard.

Even their bios seemed hard-bitten. Flipping through the guide's biographies gave a where's where of the world's toughest endurance events:

Badwater (135 miles through Death Valley in July), Spartathlon (153 miles across Greece), Marathon des Sables (160 miles across the Sahara in a week), Tor des Géants (205 miles over the Italian Alps in under six days), the Jungle Marathon (143 miles in five days), and just about every other hundred-plus miler you can imagine. These people knocked out Ironmans for warm-ups.

There I was, a broken ex–hockey player, a dad, a guy who runs before work. I'd done the TransRockies Run in Colorado, but nothing so big, nothing so far from home, nothing in such a brutal environment.

The desert was so big and I was so small.

What business do I have being here?

Yet here I was. And ten others had similarly lofty plans. Three were attempting the Grand Slam like me, aiming to run all 4 Deserts (Namib, Gobi, Atacama, and Antarctica) over the next seven months. Michele, a German, my tentmate in the Namib and the youngest-looking fifty-year-old anyone had ever seen, was a sports psychologist who specialized in mental toughness and flow-state performance. He'd run one RacingThePlanet event before. Then there was Julita, my favorite Polish *Ninja Warrior*, who was raising money for a charity that helped children with medical operations that enable them to run. And then Elise, another German, only twenty-five years old, who worked in private equity.

Beyond those, there were six more in the Grand Slam Plus (all the above events and then another "special edition" race in Finland[13]). John Bezou, naturally, having waited so long to do the series, planned to do the extra event in Finland. Mike, the vet from Miami. Rena, from Japan, who worked in financial IT. Michal from Poland nailed the first three races in 2018 but then couldn't do Antarctica—and so he looked to tackle the entire series in the 2022 Slam. Anim, a performance coach from South Africa, lived in Montreal for years and then moved on to New York state.

---

13 As so few attempt it, the race organization typically puts all the Grand Slam participants—both Grand Slam and Grand Slam Plus—in the same category.

She had done the Namib, Gobi, and Atacama in 2019, and in 2022 she was shooting for the Slam Plus.

That left Mori Mori, the nickname of Terumichi Morishita, a Japanese engineer. He was hard to miss on the start line in his fluorescent orange shirt and fluorescent yellow hat representing North Face Japan. He was my age and spoke almost no English. He was average height but huskier than you'd expect for an elite runner. He could go, and go hard—he held the course record at one of the hottest-weather 100K races on the planet, on the Japanese island of Okinawa. Not only that, in just the past fall (2021), Mori Mori pushed world record holder Harvey Lewis at Big Dog's Backyard Ultra World Championship, where he finished third overall by running over 333 miles in three days on a 4.2 mile hourly-loop course. Mori Mori had the look of a Terminator: quiet, driven, and constantly throwing off the aura that he would absolutely never, ever, ever quit.

I don't belong in a race next to this guy.

The bus stopped. "Alright, everyone, load onto the trucks now," the driver yelled over his shoulder.

We climbed into the beds of four pickup trucks, where we rode standing up the final few miles into camp.

Dunes surrounded camp completely. We walked the last stretch into camp, then under a large green sign. As we did, we heard a drum beat loudly as we approached, and the Namibian staff cheered excitedly as if we'd just won the Boston Marathon.

It was so windy we had to take off our hats or else our first race would be chasing after them. With all the gear on our backs, we approached a crescent moon–shaped array of drab olive-green army-style tents. They were numbered "1" through "12," named after ships sunk on the nearby Skeleton Coast (ours: the "SS *Charles Elliot*"). Most runners peeled off from the group to find their tents.

My three tentmates appeared. The outgoing, disheveled, absent-minded professor was Stefan from Switzerland. His English was perfect as he was born in Britain and raised in Basel. He launched into a detailed description of his work in industrial plastics (way more interesting than you'd expect). Quieter was the heavily tattooed Christopher, a smiley German, who sported a Baby Yoda patch on his shoulder and carried an enormous race pack. Then Michele, of course. For those counting, that made three German-speaking tentmates, making me the odd man out.

At the tent crescent's center, there were three firepits in a common area, in addition to three fifty-gallon barrels, cut in half, set sideways, where the local staff kept hot water kettles boiling. This operation, we were told, would run twenty-four hours a day. In addition to the tents, water was the only sustenance the race would provide. While hot water was always ready, we quickly learned there was no such thing as cold water here. Without ice or refrigeration, the "cold" water was whatever temperature the sun provided you at a given moment—our options were warm or hot.

There were few official activities, so everyone was on their own schedule. Ad hoc groups formed, a twosome at this fire, a foursome over there. Everyone got out food, sat on stools, and ate and talked. It's amazing how engaged people can be when they don't have smartphones. Absent interruption, things got really loud really quick. A constant current of conversation. It was such a social environment that it didn't bother me when my tentmates chattered away in Teutonicspeak because it provided a break from all the talking I had already been doing in camp.

As the race gathered people from around the globe, there was so much to learn about other places. Instead of name tags, the race had us all wearing flags so we knew everyone's nationality. I caught a glimpse of an Israeli runner, living in Mexico, sewing on his flag patch at the last minute while he chatted with a German girl.

I lay down at 8 PM. Lame as it sounds, in my defense, when it gets dark at 7 PM, and you're in a tent, you go to bed early. But still, I was the first one down in our tent. The wind was blowing so hard I couldn't sleep. An hour later I woke up, and it took several more attempts to fall back to sleep. Nighttime Namib seemed to be working against me. It sounded like an animal was scratching its way through the canvas, the air mattress crunched like I was sleeping on potato chips, and my super light, super cool Therm-a-Rest sleeping bag was so warm it actually made me sweaty.

The next day consisted of briefings and the all-important gear check. Sam used her bullhorn to get everyone gathered for the race brief. I sat next to Janka the German and Ivan the Dane, who I'd met on arrival. It wasn't until then that I learned Ivan was the race's oldest competitor at age sixty-eight, which blew my mind because, made entirely of ropy muscle and a visible six-pack, Ivan was also the nicest older badass I'd ever met.

The three of us talked as Sam got herself settled in front of the runners, when suddenly an enormous Namib Desert beetle crawled over Ivan's foot.

"Careful," said Janka. "It might be able to eat a Great Dane."

Sam, through her bullhorn, interjected: "Welcome to the Namib Desert, and I hope you enjoyed your time in Swakopmund. This is the sixth edition of the Namib Race being held here, and it's the sixty-seventh race held by RacingThePlanet since 2003. Everyone here has had a Covid test, including the staff, and we are one hundred percent negative."

The runners cheered. Dr. Patrick Burns, the race's head doctor—an emergency room doc at Stanford—pumped his fist to the sky.

Sam walked us through the Covid rules, provided an overview of the course, and then sent us off to gear check.

Gear check terrified me for months. It sounded so daunting, the idea that you might not have something and at the last minute wouldn't make the start line.

But seeing it play out for the first time put me at ease. Instead of the basic training–style military inspection I dreaded, it was more like a nice neighbor who comes over to offer help with a yard-sale checklist.

My assigned inspector was a volunteer—a short-haired, all-smiles South African filmmaker named Amelia, there to support her lifelong friend Anim. Amelia ticked off the list all while she made small talk in short bursts. I warmed to her immediately.

When it was all done—bags checked, calories counted, sodium plan okayed—they weighed everything.

My bag was 11.8 kilograms, about 26 pounds without water, which would bump up to over 31 pounds when the race imposed mandatory water requirements for heat (2.5 liters, or over 80 ounces). The top guys had bags nearly half my weight. My pack was too heavy.

Inspection complete, we then sealed and sent off our travel bags. These included our travel clothing and whatever else we brought on the journey beyond race-specific gear. The race secured these bags, and we were told we would get them back at the finish line. The last moments with my travel duffle felt a little panicky, as if that bag was the last thread that connected me to civilization. I finished fumbling with it, picked it up, hauled it to the collection point, and heaved it onto the pile. Now it was just me and my twenty-six pounds for the next seven days and 155 miles in the world's oldest desert.

Before bed, I found myself talking to John. He pivoted to coaching wisdom.

"In the first half—don't be an idiot," he advised. "In the second half—don't be a wimp. Since this is the first of four races, we're in the 'don't be an idiot' phase."

I mentally rephrased John's adage as I walked back to the SS *Charles Elliot*. I thought: *Be smart, be strong, be smart, be strong, be smart, be strong*...

Breathe in.

Now out.

I grasped the small blue satin square—from the baby blanket both my daughters had used—between my thumb and pointer finger. I'd pinned it to the front of my race pack.

Survive, just survive.

I wasn't sure how, but I was at the start line. In Namibia. In the Namib

Desert. My first stage would be twenty-four miles, the first of twenty-four total stages over the next seven months.

I'm at the far left of the start chute, wearing a visor, in the fog at the first stage of the Namib (and first stage of the Grand Slam year).

It was foggy; the wind had blown in from the Atlantic, which created a milky-white haze that enveloped everything. Nobody could see much in any direction.

Francois towered over the edge of the start chute, next to a half dozen other Namibian locals, who chanted along with the steady drumbeat. Francois was the race's local fixer—every bit the swarthiest Namibian there ever could be, a great bear of a man in all the best ways. He wore an old army jacket, had a full white beard, and proudly clutched a Namibian flag, quite beautiful with its green, red, and blue stripes and yellow sun.

The start chute formed a corral for the racers with two parallel walls that kept the runners together just before the starter's pistol fired. Above, the centerpiece was a fluorescent-green sign with bold black letters: "4 DESERTS NAMIB RACE 2022." More than two dozen national flags, which represented the runners' home countries, lined the chute. The great green banner was to be pulled down and rushed off to become our finish line every day. So if all went well, we would see it again soon.

As we milled around, John migrated over to me. Clean shaven, he wore a square silver bib with #4 on his chest to signify his assigned race number. (I was #6.) His Hypoxia Performance baseball cap's dirty brim, full of dried sweat and dust, held his sunglasses up. His hiking poles were broken down and slung across his front, lashed above his chest-strapped bottle. He wore a black-and-gray shemagh around his neck.

Everyone was happy. Of course we were. Nothing hurt yet. We were out of the sun on a cool morning. Except for the packs, you might mistake this for a local 5K.

But it was not.

Don't trip, I thought. *The first few steps are gonna be a rugby scrum.*

Just then, Sam, the race director, broke my thought. She pulled her bullhorn up and started the countdown.

"10, 9, 8, 7, 6, 5, 4, 3, 2, 1 . . ." Crack!

The starter's pistol fired. I couldn't see who pulled the trigger. Probably Francois; he looked like he might always be packing. All the nervous butterflies scattered from the runners and out the chute.

Time to run.

We ran into a fallen sky, through grounded clouds, which made it harder to see the pink pin flags marking the course. But the road ahead was—well, a road—so easy to follow. We took the flattened dirt road out and for the next eight miles were surrounded on all sides by a pink glow. It was some of Sub-Saharan Africa's largest salt pans, Namibia's salty white gold, flocks of flamingos in football field–sized pools boxing us in on either side.

The front runners went out fast at an eight-minutes-per-mile pace, which is hard to sustain with a pack on your back. They were geeked by the cool conditions, the exquisite scenery, the flat course, the fresh legs. I let them go ahead and stayed back at about nine minutes a mile. I might have been a rookie, but I knew enough to know the week ahead would be long.

Over time I passed one guy, then another. At the halfway mark, Checkpoint 2, the sun came out and it was brutal. I felt like an ant under a magnifying glass. That's when we hit our initial sand dunes, which were spectacular at first sight.

I felt strong and pumped my legs through the dunes all the way to mile twenty-two, but that magnifying glass from above started to sap my strength. I dropped from ten minutes per mile to eleven, to twelve, and then even slower. I kept moving forward and found the stage distance longer than advertised. We did an extra mile, for a little over twenty-five total. I slumped across the finish line in fifth place to the welcoming beat of the race drums.

I felt lightheaded, my hands tingled, my leg muscles twitched. I walked straight to the medical staff. I told them everything I could about the day, details on my sodium consumption and the precise amount of water I'd had (three liters). My visual acuity was still sharp, so at least that was working. I was talking to one of the doctors when Sam left the finish area and came over.

"Hey, Matt—you okay?" she asked.

"I've been better, but I've been way worse too," I said. "This is just me being careful."

She made eye contact with the doctor, looked back at me, and smiled, saying, "Okay, rest up, big day tomorrow."

Unsaid, but fully understood, was Sam's concern. She was the one I'd worked with for months to get medically cleared for this race, and she'd even put me in touch with Dr. Burns, the head race doctor, to make sure the medical staff was prepared for any kidney-related issues.

And now, on the very first stage, I looked salt crusted and feeble at the finish. Not good.

I sat with the medical staff for an hour. One of the docs had run the race before, so he peeked in my pack and offered tips. When he found my Clif Shot Bloks—a cube-shaped gummy and one of my favorite race foods—he lectured me.

"Dude, you know these Shot Bloks are full of fluid, so they're really heavy to carry, right?"

"Uh, you know, first time here," I said. "I've got a lot to learn."

It didn't feel good, but he was right. I left the medical area and walked over to our newly formed tent city. Every day while we ran, the staff took down our tents, along with the start/finish chute and green banner, and moved them all to the new finish area. When I got in I spotted the four guys who came in ahead of me. The common denominator was that they all had way lighter packs than me. I was carrying an extra gym plate's worth of weight, at least.

Right then I gained a new appreciation for the lesson I taught West Point cadets from 2012 to 2015, that "no plan survives contact with the enemy." It's a rephrasing of Helmuth von Moltke's writing from 1871 that I included in my military strategy course for my cadets who would soon graduate to become lieutenants. My race pack represented my "plan," and now that plan had met the "enemy" in the first stage. And my plan was way off, so I needed to shed every ounce possible.

I opened my bag and got ruthless. I threw out a pair of socks (the packing list said three, but I'd brought a fourth), a shirt, and my favorite visor of all time (sorry, Team USA). Then I focused even smaller. I threw out every unnecessary dry-toothpaste tablet, squeezed out half my lip balm tube, pitched most of my wet wipes (mental note: wet wipes were the heaviest, stupidest thing to bring here, like carrying a damp brick), and I even cut unnecessary straps off my pack. If it didn't hold salt or calories, I didn't want it.

I started to come back to life, and in the early evening I walked over to the porta johns to find a locked door and waited my turn. A few minutes later, Dudu from Israel, who finished ahead of me earlier in the day, walked out. I opened the door to what can only be described as an all-brown Jackson Pollock. Now I know where he got his nickname.[14]

An ugly end to an ugly day.

It would be hard to imagine a less restful environment than our tent city. The generator hummed at all hours. There were three toilets for a hundred people, which meant thousands of bathroom door slams daily. There was a never-ending party at the campfire because everyone, having spent most of their day running alone, made up for lost social time there.

Not to mention that you were never on the same cycle as your tentmates. Nobody went to the bathroom at the same time; nobody ate at the same time. The environment maximized chaos and minimized comfort.

I couldn't sleep. I mean, I really could not sleep. My younger brother Rob used to tell us he never slept when he was a kid, because all he remembered was closing his eyes and then—*poof*—he was awake. This was different. I looked at my watch so much it felt like I was counting all the numbers around the clock until morning. But at least I was horizontal and resting, which was something.

The second day in the Namib, we lined up just as we had the day before, under the same green banner. I rubbed my blue blanket square.

Sam fired the same starter's pistol, and we were back in the saddle. Stage 2, about twenty-six miles.

---

14 Of course that's not really where he got his nickname, but I think you get the point.

I started slow, in seventh place or so, and I even plugged in my tiny music player so I could chill out and slow my roll. I needed to because we knew today would be hotter and longer. I drank more water and took my time in the aid stations to make sure I got down everything I planned to consume. That's the tough thing about these races—you wished you had more, but unless you consumed future calories, which put you at risk for future stages, you had to stick to what you'd scheduled.

Today I also made the decision to wear my full desert cap with neck cover. Yesterday my pack pulled my shirt down just a bit, and the spot where my neck met my back got badly sunburned. I had slathered on what seemed like plenty of sunscreen there, but, like the sand, the sun got everywhere.

I did these things because the desert had already put fear into me. Everywhere on the sand I saw random detached claws, scraps of lizard skin, bones of dead things I was absolutely sure were harder to kill than me. These were ever-present, in-my-face reminders that the desert routinely ends lives. Fortune may favor the bold; the vultures get the unprepared. So I did what I could to be prepared.

It was "dune" day, which sounded like a lovely day trip. It's why a lot of people visit the Namib Desert—and a big part of why they filmed one of the *Mad Max* movies here. But dune climbing was vicious. Life teaches you to trust your feet to stay in place when you put them on the ground, but dunes throw all that off. You climb and climb and climb, and for all that effort you get inches of progress. Two steps forward, slide back. Two steps forward, slide back. Every step plunged me into the sand up to midcalf or deeper, bogged me down, and sometimes I crawled on my hands and knees. And to run *down* a dune—that day we ran down one several stories high—was thrilling for a nanomoment until you felt the hot sand kick up your backside, and every sand grain found its way into your shirt and shorts and shoes.

A great dune in the Namib Desert. From its peak, we ran straight down the steepest part.

Over time I picked off the guys in front of me until I slotted into fourth. The last one I overtook, at about mile twelve, was Mike from Miami. I saw him from quite a distance. He wore a lot of red, which stood out against the desert. As a gesture of good will, I tapped him on the shoulder and gave him a thumbs-up as I passed.

His hair-trigger, angry growl response was immediate: "Don't blow your wad on day two!"

I took it as frustration, a rough day. Especially after my day the day before, I knew what that felt like. Still, I couldn't shake it off for several miles. When I stopped at Checkpoint 2, mile fifteen, he arrived, so he was right behind me. I kicked on. I was angry. I didn't want his negative ass anywhere near me.

A strong wind picked up the last two miles into camp. Flying particles clung to my wet bottle caps, so I licked sand every time I sipped water, and the grit migrated to my molars until ultimately I was chewing sand.

As I crested what seemed like an endless sea of dunes, I broke.

When will this be over?

It's a cruel little game RacingThePlanet likes to play—they make sure you can't see the finish line and camp until you're right on top of it. You run and run and run, and the distance tells you that you're getting closer and closer and closer. But they keep it hidden from view. At this point of the day I just wanted it to be over.

André 3000 rescued me.

Outkast's "B. O. B. (Bombs over Baghdad)"—featuring André 3000's ultra-fast vocals— came onto my old-school mini music player, flooded my ears, and it was this shot of adrenaline for a few minutes that kick-started some last little leftover gear. I grinned as wide as my face could stretch.

As the song ended, I heard real-life drums pick up—the finish line! I crossed it and saw Sam smile just as much as me and my Outkast.

"Well done, Matt, well done!" Sam exclaimed. "Great day!"

Her enthusiasm made me wonder how worried she was. *Did Sam think I was going to die out there?*

Mike's day was worse. He finished over thirty minutes behind me, which meant he really slowed down after I saw him last.

I walked to my tent. It was midday, so the sun was right above us, and I was dying to get out of the scorching white heat. But our tents were full of stale air and even hotter than outside. Still, I decided to take the trade: To get myself out of the sun's intense rays, I accepted the warmer air inside.

I took my shoes off to discover the desert had given me a gift. The two toes next to each big toe had enormous blisters. Since I got in earlier than most of the other runners, I walked over to the medical tent, where they knew me pretty well already. Dr. Burns worked to puncture the pressure out, a process I was well acquainted with (having previously chosen to have my right big toenail surgically removed).

I slowly walked back to my tent and saw John crying. I patted him on the back and he sniffled, "I got some messages from the race system that hit me in the feels." The race was so remote it used a satellite internet system to relay e-messages with well-wishes from loved ones back home.

As much as the messages, the tears must've been from the exertion, which seemed strange, because for bodies that craved salt and water, the release of salty tears must only be for true emotional earthquakes. Or the sheer physical effort unlocked something inside, broke the seal on feelings that couldn't come out otherwise.

By the time I reached my tent and meager pack and pile of belongings, I sat down, pulled out a meal bar, mixed a recovery drink, and, before my first bite, started to weep. I missed my family. I missed my girls. If this were Mexico, I'd have filled a cenote.

I've felt this kind of eruption before. It started in late 2014 when Rachel found Grace, then three years old, unconscious, face blue, on the living room floor. Rachel called for paramedics immediately. I arrived just behind, and then Grace was rushed to the emergency room, her small body stabilized by a backboard brace. The diagnosis followed soon after. Grace had a seizure condition.

A few weeks later the Army sent me unaccompanied orders to South Korea, which meant I had to leave Rachel with both our newborn daughter, Georgie, and Grace's new seizure condition. Rachel then dealt with multiple ER visits for one daughter over the entire next year, all alone, with a baby in tow.

The separation was excruciating. My body was in one place, my heart in another. The little things were the worst, like the video calls that went wrong. We thought it would be nice to set up a "good night" video call for Grace, and it was, right up until she asked, "Daddy, will you be home tomorrow?" Those six words drove six knives into my chest.

I wrote every day, without exception, one letter for Rachel and one postcard for the girls. In the letter to Rachel I would place a small bead in the envelope. We each had a jar at the start of the year. My jar held 365 beads and hers was empty. The emptier mine got, the fuller hers got, the closer we got to being back together. Because the girls were so young, I would draw a postcard that only a grade school art teacher could love. I just wanted them to know—to *feel*—that I was still with them, even if in a paper-thin postcard kind of way.

Time passed, I came home from Korea, and not long after I got back home, one night, we all sat at the dinner table. Rachel started asking Grace questions about numbers and colors. I was the last one to realize what was happening: Grace was seizing. I didn't know.

Rachel started telling me what to do, "Carry Grace to the couch, lay her on her side . . ."

While doing that, I could actually see Grace drift away. She went limp and started shaking. I was at the height of helplessness, like I was just sitting there watching her drown.

The worst part, by far, was not knowing what to do. If it wasn't for Rachel, I don't know what would have happened, and I was so grateful to be with someone so competent, capable, caring. At the same time, I felt like a complete failure as a father, for being gone for so long and then not knowing what to do when it mattered the most. Grace didn't need words or cartoons, she needed someone who knew what to do in that moment, and I let her down.

I was running the next morning, and as I turned toward home, that failure nearly knocked me down. I doubled over, hands to face, and thought the worst of myself.

What good am I?

What use am I?

I never got over that feeling. In that moment, I would have traded anything for Grace's seizures to go away.[15] That thought clicked later when

---

15 We are incredibly lucky that, years later, Grace did grow out of her seizure condition.

I realized I was born with a built-in silver bullet—two healthy kidneys and I only needed one—so it made all the sense in the world to fire it. Because there was nothing I wouldn't have given to fire a silver bullet like that for Grace. And someone else's "Grace" was out there, right then—just substitute "kidney failure" for "seizure disorder."

I knew what it was to fail Rachel, to fail Grace, to fail Georgie. (I still feel it now.) And while I wasn't what they needed me to be, when they needed me to be—the kidney donation and this race in the Namib felt, to me, like something I *could* do.

Maybe.

As the sun started to set at the end of Stage 2 in the Namib, I felt a little better, a little steadier. The trouble was, when you felt good there, you knew it couldn't last. Every finish line was the starter's pistol for the next stage. There was no time to enjoy a day that went well, because you had to get ready for tomorrow. A new course. A new chance to hurt—or to fail. Your mind never stopped thinking about what was to come.

Late in the day, my new German friends provided some education and entertainment. As I walked across camp, I looked over to the medical tent and saw Elise, the youngest of the Grand Slam class, literally lose all ten of her toenails. They peeled all ten off. As in, she had toenails and the Namib Desert took them. I watched as the medical staff taught her to slowly drill an 18-gauge needle directly down into her toenail to release the blood under the nail's surface. I made a note of the technique for my next toenail peel.

From that yuck, I walked back over to the tent. Stefan and Christopher were near the front flap. Michele was inside, naked, just sort of walking around, as he tended to do.

As I approached they were talking in English with thick German accents. Laughing too.

Christopher pointed to the tent's sign, the one that said "SS *Charles Elliot*."

"Yah, yah, of course," he said, "zey give ze *SS* tent to ze Germans!"

I laughed. It helped a little.

Same green banner above the start line. Sam held up the same starter's pistol and bullhorn. Stage 3, roughly twenty-four miles.

I looked around the start line. Everyone hurt everywhere. We started thirty minutes earlier today than the previous days, which cut down recovery time. My smart-ass smartwatch told me, "You will recover fully in 1.9 days."

The start chute seems bigger, I thought. Emptier. Four runners dropped out of the race last night, so there was, in fact, more elbow room in the chute. Athletic tape was more prevalent, poking outside shirts, up and down legs. My tentmate Stefan had the biggest blister in all of camp—which was saying something—bigger than the biggest grape I'd ever seen. On his toe. And Michele too: both of his second toes in from the pinky side looked like they'd sprouted another toe each. Gross.

On this start line, scanning the others, I felt tired and drained. Worse, I was losing my ability to swallow, due to all the sand chewing, which made it harder to get the one thing I was most desperate for: calories.

I thought of the girls, again, touched the blue blanket square, again, and Sam fired the pistol, again.

We went. Again.

The course description called this stage "The Vast Open Namib Desert." This was where I met the real Namib and saw its nickname, "the land God made in anger," right up close.

People who live around there talk of two winds. The life-giving cold westerly, from the Atlantic Ocean, which generates the fog we had for the first stage. Then there's the life-sucking hot easterly that comes from the far-away Kalahari Desert, speeding up until it creates a cross between a blow-dryer and a blowtorch.

We ran into the latter wind today. Most of the day I saw nothing but upper-half blue sky, bottom-half brown ground. The race guide's epic spin described this as a view "where you can admire the infinite horizons" and that we'd "enjoy the vast Namibian desert views!"

But that was just it. There was nothing out there as far as my eye could see. And my eye couldn't even look that far, because the wind picked up and that Kalahari import blasted me full in the face. I trudged on.

Then, truly in the middle of nowhere, I saw it. This blob of tangled, twisted green leaves. A Welwitschia plant. And then another. The race guide mentioned it but nothing was as cool as seeing one in real life.

Not because they're beautiful. They're not. Not because they smell good or do anything cool, like catch flies or something. But because in a land of endless death, they live a deathless life. Welwitschias are a plant comprised of the leaves that live the longest in the entire plant kingdom. Some are said to be 3,000 years old. Their Afrikaans nickname is "two leaves that cannot die," because, fittingly, they have two leaves and can live for millennia. The plant world's ultimate survivors.

And here I was, surviving too—sort of—moving forward through a blast furnace, pack on my back, pounding out miles on yet another marathon-distance day. I thought in terms of miles and minutes, and this nasty little green guy on the ground was in it for dozens of human forevers.

I pushed on, a long straightway where I knew Michele was behind me, but I didn't care to look back. All I could think to do was force the next foot forward. The road ascended, ever so slightly into Checkpoint 3, our last, at a junction where we turned left into the Moon Valley.

The Moon Valley is a Namibian mash-up of California's Death Valley and South Dakota's Badlands. Short, spiky white-and-gray rocks randomly shoot up from the ground. Once we got on the trail that zagged and zigged through those two- and three-story rocks, we were in a solid fortress—no getting out.

I ran the descent into the valley, and because it was downhill, it felt good. Make that great. For two reasons. First, a down after a long up feels super. Then, the valley's rock walls shielded me, mercifully, from the blowing hot air.

Or so I thought. Out of the furnace and into the frying pan.

I ran on, cut in different jagged directions, snaked my way through the rocky maze. There weren't any more aid stations, it was just me striding closer to the finish. It was eerie; I was all alone in what felt like an endless canyon, and I knew if I came into contact with an animal threat there was no escape.

I focused on what I could see. I missed what I couldn't see.

I was roasting. Without me knowing—the temperature in the sun at that moment was 55 degrees Celsius, 131 degrees Fahrenheit. I just kept going because that was all that was left in my mind, all I could think to do, all I was capable of doing.

Approaching a checkpoint, Stage 3 in the Namib Desert.

One step forward.

Next step forward.

Repeat.

I hit the end of the maze and emerged to what looked like a larger canyon, a gap between big rock walls with some vegetation. I knew by my GPS watch I must've been getting close to the end. As I approached the edge of the green, I saw a pink pin flag trail that took me into the bush. But this wasn't a normal leafy bush, this was the Namib, so every branch scraped skin.

I weaved my way through a forest of sharp things. I started to wobble, to weaken. Inexplicably, I stopped running and walked. Just walked. As if I wasn't in control anymore. Someone else had my body's remote control and flipped the switch to autowalk. I couldn't find the next pink flag marking the race route, so I just tried to find my way out of the green so I could see something, anything, besides spiky bushes.

That's when I heard them. *The drums!*

I got clear of the bush, walked on, and spotted what looked like a dirt ramp up to the finish line. I walked up it, the last few meters, and there waiting for me was what appeared to be the entire race staff and Dudu and Reinhold. Everyone had water and they started drowning me and taking my shoes off. Normally the staff doesn't provide runners with ice, but that day they made an exception. Big Francois became my God of Ice and Cold when he wandered up with a bucket of the coldest ice and water that had ever touched my skin.

I couldn't speak. It all felt so good and so bad, all at once.

I finished fourth.

Sam called off the race after the first dozen runners came in to the finish. They stopped people at the last checkpoint before the Moon Valley and drove them in trucks to the finish.

I didn't collect my thoughts (or my lost sock) for several hours. Hard as the day was, it felt like validation. On the hottest day I had ever run, my single kidney did its job. It did not hold me back.

The overnight was torture. I couldn't eat. I couldn't drink. I couldn't rest. It was so hot. I aimed for two of three. I sat on top of my sleeping bag and nibbled at food and took SaltStick capsules and forced down as much (warm) water as I could take.

I was not stopping. I was not done. Not yet.

The next morning and I was back under the green sign again, tapped the blue blanket square again. Sam had her bullhorn. Stage 4, twenty-four miles.

I didn't feel good, but I was upright and ready-ish for the day.

I was also shocked. Mike from Miami wasn't on the start line. He was over by Sam, not in his race gear.

I looked over at John.

"He can't pee," John told me. "They think his kidneys aren't working."

"Shit. Seriously? Shit!" I was more than a little freaked out, worried that Mike was an omen for me. If your kidneys don't work, that's a kill shot. Maybe literally in the Namib.

In truth, pre-race, I didn't really think too hard about this worst case. While I thought about the risk of death from time to time, the thought that I might seriously damage my remaining kidney never really crossed my mind. Well, that is, not until I saw Mike.

But it didn't much matter in that moment. I had a race, and it was just seconds before the gun fired again—for the fourth time in four days.

Sam pulled the trigger, and I forgot Mike and just went. We went into the Moon Valley again, but today was cooler, and we got to climb up and out of the bottom of that rocky frying pan onto the ridgeline above, which gave us 360-degree views.

Running up to a ridgeline view of the Moon Valley in the Namib Desert.

I ran with Michele most of the day, both of us depleted from the day before, and after the last checkpoint I dropped him and ran alone for the last hour. At this point I was up an hour on him for the race, a strong but not certain lead as we headed into The Long March the next day.

I crossed the line again in fourth—behind Reinhold, Mori Mori, and Dudu—and this finish provided me a peek into how they did it. I sat down under some shade with Reinhold and Dudu, and they opened their packs and minds to me.

Reinhold especially. He showed me his mandatory carry multi-tool. He'd taken apart the smallest Swiss Army knife you've ever seen and stripped everything but the blade. The packing list said three pairs of socks, so he had a regular pair of running socks and then two pairs of the superthin, tiny socks that women sometimes wear under high heels. Some would say he's skirting the spirit, if not the letter, of the rules, but in the end it was his risk to take. If his regular socks ripped, his only recourse would be those little foot condoms.

I proudly pulled out my sleeping bag, stuffed tightly into its stuff sack. It was the very first thing I bought for the race. *Ta-da!*

Reinhold frowned. He looked at my stuff sack with disapproval and said in a strong Swiss accent, "Matt, why do you have a bag . . . for another bag?"

I couldn't respond. Dynamite went off between my ears. *Ka-blooey!*

It all made sense. The dust pushed away. Everything went clear.

"Oh! You mean," I said several moments later, "that you think of a stuff sack as extra weight? So where—how—do you put your sleeping bag in your race pack?"

Reinhold showed me that his sleeping bag went right in the race pack and filled in all the gaps and spaces. The sleeping bag's stuff sack, then, was truly unnecessary weight. I saw how every one of his hundreds of tiny decisions added up, gram by gram, ounce by ounce, until he carried half the weight I had in my bag.

Dudu lost interest in the conversation. Low on food, he wandered off because something caught his eye.

"Calories!" Dudu shouted. Then again, we heard, "Calories!"

Reinhold and I looked over and saw Dudu clutching a small bird in both hands. He was grinning ear to ear, shirtless, bronzed, basically a Bedouin in his element. The intense desert sun didn't seem to bother Dudu, a geographic advantage born of his home in the Israeli desert.

We laughed and I looked back to Reinhold to ask about his pack. Mine had been rubbing my shoulders and lower back really bad. It was my back, so I couldn't actually see how bad it was, but I sure could feel it. I knew I would have to start from scratch after this race; there was just no way this pack punishment could continue.

We talked for another minute. I walked over to my tent, made my dehydrated meal, and got horizontal. We expected fifty-one miles the next day in The Long March.

I glanced out through the open tent flap at Dudu as he smiled, opened his hands, and let the bird take flight.

I wish I could fly away too, I thought.

The Long March morning. I did not want to wake up.

Clearing camp before The Long March in the Namib Desert.

An hour before the day's start, camp looked like an army aid station. Everyone wounded. The sky was blue and the rocks were golden as the sun climbed, so it still felt almost cool. But we knew the heat was inbound because early that morning Sam told us we would do a mandatory stop for three hours, from 12 noon to 3 PM, to get everyone out of the extreme heat. The race wasn't taking any chances after the other day.

My list of concerns had grown since last night. My back was worse than I thought. At the top, the skin had rubbed through and bled, so I asked John to tape it up. And my lower back was so raw it felt hot and lumpy when I touched it. My only option was to get through the first half hour of pain until both went numb.

Time disappeared. I looked up and I was under the green banner. Sam had her bullhorn again.

I stood next to John in the start chute.

"Dude, what is that you keep touching?" John asked.

"This?" I had the thumb-sized blue fabric between my fingers and twisted it toward him. "I cut this square from the baby blanket both my girls used. It's good luck, for when I lose it. When I need what I don't have."

After a pause, "I need it now. Bad."

Just like that, the starter's pistol fired. We were off. Again.

Michele was my mark. He was an hour down, and as long as I kept him within sight I would hold my place. Which was fine because I thought he was about where I was physically. We ran together, and for a while I drifted off mentally, my eyes got lazy, and I stopped hunting the next pink pin flag.

"Have you seen a flag?" Michele shouted over to me.

"No." His question startled me. "I guess I haven't." I was embarrassed; I should have been keeping up.

We ran on for another few hundred meters and realized we were off track. We missed a turn.

It took us an extra couple miles to double back. By the time we got back on course, Vicki, the women's leader, had caught up and we ran as a pack. There was a long way to go, we were all tired, and it felt better to run together.

We crossed a long open stretch where there was nothing in any direction and we could see for three infinities. Eventually we spotted Checkpoint 3, but it took at least two of those infinities to get there.

When we arrived, a race official told us it was so close to 12 noon that we could elect to take our rest here at Checkpoint 3 or run on to Checkpoint 4 and take the rest period there. Either way we would get a three-hour official race time "pause." I immediately decided to take my rest here, but Michele and Vicki were both inclined to push on to Checkpoint 4.

Then, a moment later, the same race official asserted we *ought* to run on to Checkpoint 4, because they anticipated there would be a large group of runners coming in soon, and they only had so much shade and water at Checkpoint 3.

Michele and Vicki ran off. I stuck to my guns. I needed to hold, no matter what the pressure. But this choice created a new problem. I was pacing against Michele, keeping him within sight. At this point he'd run on ahead. So I could either freak out and chase him now, or trust in myself that I could take this rest and then run him down later to hold on to fourth place overall.

I chose the latter.

I stayed at Checkpoint 3 for my three hours. We were on a high point, and a hot wind came in strong that blew away everything not tied down. A volunteer covering her mouth from flying sand with a Namibian flag gaiter shot me with a water spray mist to cool me down.

At Checkpoint 3 during extreme heat pause in the Namib Desert.

At the same checkpoint during heat pause.

As I rested, so many runners showed up—John, Anim, Elise, most of the rest of the Grand Slammers, and then some.

Just before 3 PM, I got up and ran on, alone.

When I reached Checkpoint 4, Michele and Vicki were gone, having taken their rest there, but waiting for me there was the legendary RacingThe-Planet 4 Deserts Coke. The race has become famous for giving runners a Coca-Cola at some late stage of the race. Runners never know when it'll come. And for us, the surprise was at Checkpoint 4. I downed the entire twelve ounces—the sugar water my lips dreamed of all week—in under five seconds.

I ran on, by myself, for hours and hours, past abandoned buildings, past a river and a small lake, under a highway, over hills, through cracks in rocks, until the sun set and the heat of the day vanished.

It was dark when I approached the finish line thirteen hours after I started—ten hours of running—just shy of fifty miles (including the two extra Michele and I did together).

Dudu was waiting at the finish line, pulled my pack off, and helped me to my tent. I was too tired to say much except "thank you." I ate a snack, crawled into my sleeping bag, and tried my best to sleep while the finish-line drums pounded and pounded and pounded.

The drums still pounded when I woke the next morning. Sheer exhaustion was the only reason I got any sleep. Most of the runners had yet to finish The Long March. Today was built into the schedule as a buffer, to allow runners extra time to complete the longer stage. I wandered over to Sam, who told me that Michele gained a few minutes on me yesterday on The Long March, but I was still nearly an hour ahead of him overall. Tomorrow's final stage would be a jog to the finish, around six miles, so he couldn't catch me. Unless I died.

Which seemed a possibility right then. I had just run fifty miles with a pack on through the desert. My body screamed for calories.

I didn't have calories.

Well, I had some, but not nearly enough. I had less than 1,000 calories left in my bag to survive the day and start the next. A 420-calorie breakfast cookie, a 245-calorie recovery drink, two meat bars totaling 210 calories, and a 90-calorie olive oil packet. That was it.

I nibbled, lay down a while, nibbled, lay down a while. I moved as little as possible. I once read that in the course of a lifetime, humans eat the weight equivalent of six elephants. I'd have taken down two at this point.

My stomach made noises it should not make. Worse than organs moving in your gut.

I was eating myself, and I knew it, and there was nothing I could do but survive to run six more miles tomorrow.

Green banner, check. Bullhorn, check. Tap the blue, check. One more time. Stage 6.

This time, Sam started us in two batches. Slower runners went an hour ahead, and those at the front of the pack departed later. That way everyone would arrive at the finish line more bunched together.

I thought about this stage like a jog. A glorified fun run. No matter what happened, I wasn't going to catch Dudu (he was in third overall), and I wasn't going to fall back behind Michele (who was in fifth).

But Mori Mori had something else in mind. He had run this race over five hours faster than me to this point, an hour faster than me each day. He had demonstrated every kind of running superiority over me. Yet he was still in second overall, behind Reinhold, by about five minutes.

To make up five minutes over six miles is really hard under normal circumstances. Out here it was downright crazy to even think about, let alone attempt. But when Sam started our group on that final stage, Mori Mori launched out, which forced Reinhold to push too. The rest of us looked out at the two of them—Mori Mori in particular—in awe. It was the ballsiest, most tenacious thing I had ever seen a runner do.

Nope, I thought. I jogged my way in.

I heard the sound of the ocean off in the distance, and I knew the finish line was getting closer. I started to sniffle, to tear up, to think about the week, about how hard it was and how many times I thought I would never get to these final steps.

And here they were.

I thought about Georgie, about Grace, about Rachel—gripping the blue square like it was a button that could teleport me home, if only in my mind.

I heard the drums and saw the green banner and a huge group of people. I ran to the drums, to the green, to the crowd, and as I crossed the finish, two Namibian women wearing traditional outfits, handmade grass skirts, without tops and with loads of beaded necklaces, walked toward me as I approached. One had something shiny, a medal with a lanyard, so I could tell they were going to put it around my neck when I reached the line.

There were all these people grouped near the finish and everyone was smiling and the two women were smiling and one put the lanyard up and over my head and now I had my finisher's medal and I smiled too and I did what I always do at a finish line when someone puts a medal around my neck.

I leaned in to hug her.

But then I snapped out of it and realized she wasn't wearing a top—she backed up and said "No, no, no!" and looked at me as if to say, *Are you crazy!*

I felt like such an asshole, but I was too weak to care.

I wasn't happy, but I felt relief. Satisfied. I was just glad I'd made it—that I did what I set out to do and more. To finish fourth overall at this race, under these conditions, felt meaningful. And now I just wanted to be home.

Pain crowded out any true joy.

I found John and we walked a few blocks across Swakopmund to our hotel, where our travel bags awaited. John and I had rooms down the hall from one another, so together we dragged our bags to our respective rooms.

I realized the athletic tape on my upper back needed to come off, so I asked him to help me.

"You know, you might want to let it sit under the water in the shower first," John coached me, "before we pull it off. It might rip."

But I was impatient, definitely not thinking straight. "Don't worry about that, let's just get this stuff off."

I put my bags in my room. With my hotel room door open, standing in the entryway, at the midpoint of a long hallway of rooms, John and I lowered our centers of gravity and braced ourselves.

He pulled. Hard. Really hard.

"*Ahhhhhhh!!!*" I yelled louder than I thought possible. People up and down the hallway came out of their hotel doors and craned their necks to see what was wrong. Two other runners—Carole from Luxembourg and Doreen from the US—were in the room across the hall and rushed out almost instantaneously.

I looked at the tape. Two chunks of bloody back flesh were stuck to it. I gagged a little, then apologized to Carole and Doreen. John looked sorry.

Before he could speak, I told him, "My bad, man, you warned me, not your fault."

I closed the hotel room door. I was alone for the first time in a week. I stepped toward the full-length mirror on the wall next to the bathroom. I turned around and looked over my shoulder.

For the first time I saw the damage to my back. The upper part was literally flayed, blood dripped from what had just opened up. The bottom protruded so much it looked as though someone had implanted a small pillow under the skin. It looked like a red fanny pack when I turned sideways. Everywhere was scorching hot to the touch.

I cried. All I could think, over and over and over, was—*How can I do another in five weeks? And then two more?*

I felt hopeless.

I can't do this again. I'm not going to make it.

ACTION THIS DAY

In war, no plan or assumption survives contact. Like life, it's just too big with too many variables to ever fully get right. You just want to be less wrong than your adversary. Recalculation speed when in the fight always matters more than pre-combat plans. Adapt and survive.

And just as much as you should be prepared to change your plan and your assumptions, you should be prepared to change yourself. The Namib Race changed me, of course, by forcing me to cut weight and rethink my definition of "necessary." I adapted and barely survived.

What are your key, load-bearing assumptions?

What pre-planned weight might you have to throw off?

Chapter Five

SHOOT THE WOLF CLOSEST TO THE SLED

Every comfort requires sacrifice.

May 9, 2022
O'Hare International Airport
Chicago, Illinois

W*hat the fuck what the fuck what the fuck.*

I was running. Again. I shouldn't have been. But I was. And that made me really mad because everything hurt.

Not only that, I was running in jeans through Chicago's O'Hare International Airport to catch my next flight. Jeans that pressed against my now-distended-and-bruised-and-bloated lower back, which created the world's weirdest muffin top. Not cool.

I felt every eye on me. I caught a glimpse of myself in a display mirror as I ran past a shop in the terminal. I looked ridiculous.

I nearly knocked over an older woman because my mind miscalculated what my body could do. Then I saw my gate.

"Final boarding call, last call, Colorado Springs," I heard the gate attendant announce as I flipped my ticket's barcode face down on the scanner. She smiled and said, "Welcome, Mr. Cavanaugh. Have a great flight."

I wasn't even halfway down the hallway to the plane when I heard them close the door to the terminal behind me.

When I got to my seat, I slumped, sweaty and tired but happy because I had narrowly avoided another full day trapped in an airport.

Thirty-six days until departure for my next race.

Upon returning home, I felt so broken I didn't run for a week. I called Jason Koop, my coach, confided in him how much the Namib had taken out of me, and laid bare my doubts about doing another in five weeks. I didn't say "I can't" during the call, but I sure didn't utter any "I cans" either. The Namib beat the confidence out of me.

What if I don't have any ammo left? You don't show up at a gunfight without bullets. I learned that the hard way in Iraq.

I knew how deep my wounds were. Hard to forget when my shirt still clung to the sticky ooze on the edge of my not-yet-fully-formed scabs.

Jason talked me down from the ledge a little. He said not to worry about taking some time off—assured me it was fine. "Fitness is stubborn," he said, making sure I understood that after the week I'd just had, my body's motor wouldn't degrade so soon.

In fact, a little rest was exactly what I needed. My lower back injury turned into a massive black bruise, and then the blood from that bruising descended into the top of my butt. (Hence the muffin-top thing.)

I wondered, *Is any of this worth it? I've written over a dozen blog posts on the races, and they don't seem to be gaining an audience or any traction. What if this doesn't inspire anybody else to donate at all?*

The next race was to be held in the Gobi Desert, but as both Mongolia and China were not permitting travelers due to the pandemic, former

Soviet Georgia became the replacement race. With only five weeks between Namib and the race in Georgia, my whole focus was to cut weight. I accepted that I had less control over how quickly my body would heal, but the factor that I could control was my pack weight.

Reducing it became my priority.

"Shoot the wolf closest to the sled, Cadet Cavanaugh. Shoot the wolf."

He taught chemistry my freshman year at West Point. A short officer who wore the highest and tightest high-and-tight at a place known for them. He had a habit while walking around during our labs—he always advised me to focus on my first priority. Zero in on the first threat first. It works for academics because it helps a student eliminate the inessentials, and for me, as a not-terribly-science-oriented student, that level of focus was necessary. It also works more broadly in life, because distraction is a modern disease. Smartphones have become attention bombs, set to blow at any moment, forcing users to the immediate at the expense of the important.

I learned that focused-priority lesson the hard way when I took the Law School Admission Test (LSAT). I had recently returned from Iraq and thought I'd take a crack at it. But I hadn't prepared nearly enough and was all over the mental map. When the day came, I blew it, didn't finish all the questions, not even through guessing. My head hurt so bad I went home, ate an entire pizza, and tried to wash my mental breakdown away with a mind-numbing, cauldron-sized whiskey and Coke.

I eventually figured it out, and in the time gap between the Namib and Georgia, I'd never seen such a big bad wolf so clearly. I had to knock down my priority swiftly and accurately, before my pack weight could pull me and the entire racing year down with it.

The learning process to reduce weight for Georgia started back in the Namib. While I listened to Reinhold, I scribbled a list on the race's paper course guide, mostly of lighter-weight substitutions, with a header "Ways to cut weight":

- Food swaps, add in nuts
- At-rest pants (Raidlight?)
- Different sandals, lighter
- Can I get by with less DripDrop?
- No extra hat, use lighter hat
- TP wipes over one pound!
- Smaller light
- Swiss Army knife cut down
- Tiny socks
- Small fold mirror (cut?)
- Dried tomato soup
- Hard bottles
- SanDisk 8 GB (tinier music player)
- Goal Zero Flip 12 (battery)
- Therm-a-Rest pillow and new mat
- Montane rain jacket
- Raidlight pack 24L + 4L front
- e+Lite, Bindi, from Petzl
- Camping TP, dried, rehydrate
- Xero shoes, DIY pair

I started with calories. I had two objectives: Bring less food and bring denser food. Less food is obvious enough. The race requirement was to bring no fewer than 14,000 calories. I had brought around 20,000 calories to the Namib. That's the hard way to cut weight: Eat less.

Then there's density. Eat different. Most nuts, like macadamias, come in at about 200 calories per ounce, which is about as dense as you can get and meant you could cram 3,200 calories into a single pound if you could stick solely to such dense food. That figure was more theoretical than practical because that "ideal" didn't account for necessary calories that can never get so dense, like drink mixes that carry critical electrolytes. Still, in an ideal world, with the densest food possible, you could hit the 14,000-calorie mark in under 4.5 pounds (around two kilograms) of food.

When I looked back on my Namib Race, the food I carried was

around thirteen pounds (heavier than some runners carried in total). My typical day there I consumed 3,245 calories.

The plan for Georgia was to cut my daily calories about 20 percent (635 calories per day less than the Namib). Each day I budgeted 2,610 calories, 350 mg caffeine, 6,335 mg sodium (nearly triple the standard US daily recommendation for sodium but probably appropriate for an endurance event like this).

For simplicity I planned my routine daily calories in Georgia like so: two Clif Bars, a Justin's nut butter packet, loads of Sport Beans (endurance specific jelly beans from Jelly Belly) and Honey Stinger chocolate waffles, a recovery drink, lots of DripDrop electrolyte drink mix, and then at the end of the day a single dehydrated meal. For my daily meal I chose something I could tolerate well: a green chili mac and cheese to which I would add extra salt and spice. The problem I should have anticipated—but did not—was that because I brought the same meal for every day, such a lack of variety would be bad for my appetite.

It was all guesswork, based on the thinnest of experience. Carrying your calories is a terrible guessing game. Imagine that for the entire next week you have to select all your calories right now. You have to pick today what you'll eat Tuesday morning, Thursday afternoon, and Saturday night. You have to pick it all and pick it now.

That's not just a mental challenge but a physical one as well. You cannot predict how hungry you'll feel in those moments or whether the foods you pick now will sit well with future you. You may select something that seems great, but when the time comes, it might not be what your stomach needs. And you've just got to live with it.

Weightwise, I estimated my food came to about nine pounds in my pack for Georgia. Significantly lighter than in the Namib, but still double the ideal. I needed a broader overhaul if I was going to make it in Georgia. That meant cutting gear.

Every comfort requires sacrifice. At the 4 Deserts you carry the tools of your own comfort, and so that forces you to think extra hard about what comfort you're willing to carry.

I didn't have a set goal for gear. I went one by one, item by item, and looked for ways to cut weight for each and every single item in my pack.

I started with the pack itself. The first pack I bought weighed three pounds. Right away my training eliminated that one because it did not fit well, so I chucked it even before the Namib. The pack I did wear in the Namib—again, just to *hold* my gear—weighed two pounds. That was a huge cost.

I had seen several other runners wearing Raidlight packs, made specifically for desert running. These packs minimized weight and were made of materials that could tolerate high temperatures. No waterproofing necessary, which meant they were designed for the features I needed. I opted for a twenty-four-liter backpack with a four-liter front pack attachment, because that would avoid having all the weight on my back. The backpack was about three-quarters of a pound, and the front pack about one-quarter of a pound, for a total of a pound. That first cut alone shaved a pound.

Unfortunately, even in the midst of so much subtraction, I did need one addition. I opted against a good sleeping pad in the Namib and regretted it. So I found an upgraded air-filled pad. It was heavier than the other one—costly—but I justified it because changing my pack more than covered the cost in sleep-pad weight.

I went down the required gear list, one by one, and swapped out mandatory items for lighter versions. I bought a Montane Podium pull-on rain jacket, the lightest-weight rain jacket I could find. That replacement saved me another half pound.

Then I found a do-it-yourself sandal from a company called Xero Shoes that enabled me to air out my feet around camp after each race day. Xero mailed me two pre-cut strips of überthin (4 mm) soles, then I punched a hole in each and used a video tutorial to tie strings to make a huarache sandal. They weighed nearly nothing and allowed me to cut several ounces from the other pair of sandals I had worn in the Namib. Another quarter pound lighter.

One of my biggest bonehead mistakes in the Namib was that I took pre-moistened wet wipes, basically a wet cinder block in my bag. For Georgia, I found pill-sized dry tablets that, when watered, would grow to be wet wipes for body cleaning and other like activities. Almost weightless. Another pound lighter.

One item that caught my attention on the optional part of the mandatory gear list was about dogs.

Huh? I thought, as I read the race's email:

> There are dogs along the course. We will be working to make sure they are contained and avoid any areas where we might not be able to contain them. If you are afraid of dogs, you may consider purchasing the Dog Dazer to deter them.

My experience in Iraq—only a day's drive south from where we'd be in Georgia—convinced me to take this warning seriously. I bought some dog spray, Halt dog repellent, for $11.88, threw it in my bag, in part because I'd learned the country's name, "Georgia," is derived from an old Persian word meaning "land of wolves."

Twenty days until departure for Georgia.

I had a conference in London with the United Kingdom Ministry of Defence a couple weeks before the race. I gave a talk at a beautiful old building next to the Thames River on why deterrence had failed to stop the Russians from invading Ukraine.

To get back into the US, I had to take a Covid test, a nerve-wracking experience because it was hard to fathom what might happen if I came up positive.

Of course, I allowed myself to fathom a bit, to freak out a little, to contemplate the consequences, and none of it was good. I would have been stuck in London while all my newly acquired race gear was back in the US in the few remaining days to departure for Georgia. I'd have been screwed.

The test came back negative, so I breathed a sigh of relief and boarded my flight from London back to the US on June 4.

Ten days until departure for Georgia.

After twenty-five years in uniform, including my time at West Point, my retirement from the US Army in late spring 2023 was a year away. With accumulated leave and a transition period, backing up from that date, I would be eligible to take off my uniform at the end of 2022—not long after the year's final race on Antarctica.

That forced a choice. For many years the girls followed my work out of necessity. So I offered Rachel the decision—she would determine whether we would stay in Manitou Springs, Colorado, or move into a condo we owned in Park City, Utah. She'd had an informal job offer from the professional company she began her career with, Ballet West in Salt Lake City. Moreover, her family was there. If we were to move, it made sense to do it in the summer of 2022 so the kids could start fresh in Park City at the beginning of the next school year.

Rachel mulled it over and decided we would go to Utah. In turn, that meant we had to empty our house in Manitou to make way for renters. It also meant I would be alone in an apartment in Manitou Springs for the next six months, serving out my last few months in the military before I could join them in Utah after Antarctica.

It was so sad. To leave the home we'd lived in the longest together—17 Washington Avenue. Nearly six years and it was over.

Wednesday, June 8, was our last day in the house. I did what I could to hold work back so I could be around the girls. Georgie went for a playdate at a friend's house. Grace read a pile of books on the porch.

Rachel helped me move some heavy things into my apartment on the other side of town. At about 3 PM, I took the girls to the town's old-timey arcade, where we played Skee-Ball and cashed in our tickets. Grace got a squishy animal; Georgie, a smiley yo-yo.

They left at 4 PM to drive to Utah. Next to the loaded truck, Georgie teared up and said, "I don't want you to stay, I want you to come with us." I hugged her little body, promised her I'd visit soon, in three weeks. Grace was more composed, stoic even. She had been through this more than Georgie. But her calm didn't matter much because by then I was already crying, enough to have to wipe tears aside so as not to soak her shoulder as I hugged her.

By the time I got to Rachel, my wet eyes turned into a shaking body. I felt wobbly, so when I hugged her I was doing it to hold myself upright.

I didn't know what to do with myself after the hugs, so I walked in front of the truck and tapped the hood, and then I stood aside and waved as they backed out of the driveway.

I walked inside, up the spiral staircase, the wood creaking loudly, echoing in the empty house. I went to the porch and watched as the truck stopped for a moment, Rachel said goodbye out her window to our neighbor, and then the truck pulled away and turned out of sight.

I felt empty.

But I was full of regret.

Why didn't I beg her to stay? If our relationship was on the rocks—and it was—then wouldn't it make sense to spend more time together to work it out? It felt like their leaving—Rachel especially—was just another step apart, one more step toward being broken beyond repair.

I tried to rationalize it, to hunt some silver lining, that maybe this would provide us distance enough to heal. Maybe I'd have more time to train and finish work and retire, and we'd all reconnect on the other side of the Utah state line.

But in that moment I was depleted. I walked from room to room in the house, the remnants of our lives still everywhere. In the girls' room, behind the stand-up air conditioning unit, was the stuffed moose and "Big Squishy," the way-oversized plush, armless, legless pug that Georgie adored.

I wandered into the kitchen and looked in the pantry, where I found a corkboard with tacked-up pictures of all three girls smiling back at me.

That was when 17 Washington Avenue transformed from our home to just a house.

Six days until departure for Georgia.

I started waking up at 2 AM to adjust to the time—Georgia is ten hours ahead of Colorado. It seemed hopeless because even with 2 AM wake-ups, that was still the equivalent of rising at 12 noon in Georgia.

On June 13 I ran with my new Raidlight pack for the first time. It fit fine, but because I hadn't fully loaded it, it was lighter than it would be for the race.

One day until departure for Georgia.

I woke to an email:

> Dear Racers,
>
> We are now in Georgia finalizing the course—wow, it's beautiful with so many colors, from purple flowers to dark green hills! As we have been out on the course and looking ahead to the weather for the next few

days, we have decided to make water-proof pants a mandatory equipment item.

We hope that the weather will clear up for the race but given the changing weather patterns in the world, we would rather be prepared.

See you soon in Tbilisi.

John had departed the day before so he didn't have time to react. I went to his house to see his wife, Karen, and picked up his "waterproof pants," which were really a white Tyvek suit Karen had gotten for him at a hardware store—because it was technically waterproof and had the added benefit of being especially lightweight.

Karen and I made small talk, which helped me burn some butterflies. I groused about how beat up I still felt from the Namib. She said that John was beat too.

It's a weird feeling going back to battle not knowing what's left in your magazine. The thought crossed my mind, as I drove to the airport, that I might not have much. *Heck, maybe only one round left*, I thought.

But if I shoot straight, and there's only one big wolf, one bullet's enough.

Three hours until departure for Georgia.

ACTION THIS DAY

Problems don't line up neatly. They surround us like a pack of wolves.

There's nothing we can do about that. We can't control it. But we can triage. Use our judgment. Pick off the first one. Then the next. You may not have enough ammo for all of them, but maybe you can knock enough down to deter the rest.

That's a principle worth dwelling on. Don't fear the problem—or the pack—for its size. Again, that's something you can't control. But what you can control, what you can do, is hit the first one.[16] The closest one. That act will change the remaining pack's behavior. The scenario will change, even if a little. Then, if need be, shoot the next. It's impossible to predict the impact so don't give up too early.

In sum—focus on the closest, truest threat as if your life depends on it. It just might. In my case, the threat was additional weight.

What's yours?

What's the wolf closest to your sled?

16 With all this talk of wolf shooting, it's worth mentioning: This is strictly a metaphor and no wolves were harmed in the making of this book. For the record, I like wolves.

Chapter Six

IRON SHARPENS IRON

RACE ACROSS THE MUDDIEST DESERT—THE CAUCASUS

At this point, I'm running less on training and more on faith.

June 16, 2022
Tbilisi, Georgia

I spent most of the morning walking around Tbilisi snapping pictures of beautiful graffiti on gritty old buildings in an attempt to stay awake. I linked up with John, and we climbed precisely 144 steps to the 144 Stairs Café—named, of course, for the work it takes to get so high onto the hillside. Narikala Fortress was behind us, built in the fourth century, and later given its title by the Mongols ("little fortress"). Narikala didn't look so little from up so high—the café had spectacular views over the city and the Kura River. Whether watching for marauders or sipping a latte, you could see everything from up there.

John and I talked for two hours as we looked out from 1,200 feet above Tbilisi. We'd barely spoken since he'd flayed flesh from my back in the Namib. I had been so busy with work and life, moving and packing.

It was nice to just sit and talk and enjoy the view, without having another thing to rush off to.

I hadn't realized how lonely I was. Constantly preparing for this run meant I spent all my mental bandwidth on Georgia. My family was gone, my apartment a noiseless cave.

Sitting with John was the first time since Namib I felt fully relaxed and in contact and conversation with someone I cared about and who cared about me. A brother by choice. A teammate. And bullshitting with John was the best cure for loneliness. When you're into these races and travel to what seems damn near the end of the earth, it was a great thing to know somebody from where you're from. Somebody connected to home. Somebody like John.

It was a comfort. It also made me bolder. I thought, *I can do better than just survive this race.* With help from John, Reinhold, and the others who'd helped me so far, I'd learned to endure more than before.

I survived the Namib. I can endure this race, I thought.

"There's another Grand Slammer here," John told me. "I met him last night. Ahmed. From Abu Dhabi."

Ahmed, a cop, had finished another edition of the Namib Race six months before John and I did. RacingThePlanet allowed him to use that event as part of this year's Grand Slam Plus. A super guy, he smiled all the time, was around the same age as us, and became a solid addition to our Grand Slam group.

Most of the rest were back as well: John Bezou, Rena, and Mori Mori from Japan, Julita from Poland, and Anim from the US (by way of Canada and South Africa) were there for the Grand Slam Plus. Then Elise (sporting her partially regrown toenails), Michele (my amateur nudist former tentmate), and I were there for the Grand Slam. That made nine of us Grand Slammers.[17]

---

17 Michal from Poland was not at this event because he had done a recent, previous iteration of the race that would count toward his Grand Slam.

The rest of the field was spectacular, even with the relatively late location change from the Gobi Desert to the Caucasus of Georgia. Representing twenty-three countries in all, the oldest runner was seventy-nine years old and the youngest was twenty-four. Florian from Switzerland won the Namib Race in 2019, and the race staff strongly suggested he would be the favorite to win Georgia.

"Have you met Florian?" I asked John.

"I thought I saw him," he replied, "but only a glimpse across the lobby. I heard he's really fast. Like, really fast. Faster than Reinhold; Swiss too."

With that we descended the 144 stairs back to city level, took a few side streets to walk along the Kura, and then headed back toward our separate hotels near Freedom Square, where six separate streets connected under a giant gold statue of Saint George slaying his dragon.

I spent the next day resting and reading about Georgia.

Wedged beneath the Caucasus Mountains and between the Black and Caspian Seas, just north of Turkey, Armenia, and Azerbaijan, Georgia is ancient and tough and cold and damp and full of wild dogs.

The geography is imposing, as the Caucasus Mountains to the north include some of the highest peaks in Europe that also provide a partial barrier against the Russians. That hasn't stopped several empires from invading for millennia, including the Byzantines, Persians, Mongols, Ottomans, and Russians. One local author wrote, by his count, Tbilisi ("place of the warm water," for its natural sulfur baths) had been destroyed twenty-seven times, sacked more than any other world city save for Jerusalem. Which is why, despite being the Georgian capital for 1,500 years, no royal palaces survive today. All were knocked down by invaders.

This place and its violent past have bred a remarkable culture. The written Georgian language has no known connections to any other, so it looks like nothing you've ever seen. The food is exquisite. The khachapuri, a bread, cheese, and egg blend, is equal parts familiar and distinct in its many forms. The khinkali, the Georgian take on dumplings, is exceptional (and whatever you do, don't call them "dumplings" among actual Georgians). Their Saperavi grapes, used for wine, are as good as they are old—the Georgians have a strong claim on being the first in the world to make wine.

A quick look at a map showed we would be running a few hours west of Tbilisi, beginning in the Javakheti region ("place of the Javakhs"), a name that first shows in the historical record in 785 BC.

This place is old.

Old as dirt. Old as mud. And there was plenty of it.

We left Tbilisi at 2 PM and rode for two hours by bus to Algeti National Park. The view from the window looked like rural West Virginia, a coincidental connection because Georgia is the same size as the US state. But one thing stood out.

It was the muddiest place on the planet. The race trucks were all four-wheel drives, and every single tire on every single truck spun out of control constantly.

I walked through the mud to my assigned tent (#7), named for Lake Bureti, one of the lakes we would run by this week—though it looked as if this whole place would itself soon become one big contiguous body of brown water.

I stepped through the open tent door and instantly had four eyes on me.

"No, uh ... shoes," a Japanese guy said to me in halting English. It was Hiroki, a food tech CEO from Japan. Hiroki was next to Mori Mori. They had arrived in the group ahead of me and had already claimed tent spots.

"Okay, of course, I'll get them off." I looked down at my shoes; they were a little wet, not too muddy. Both Hiroki and Mori Mori were deeply concerned about tracking mud in the tent. It would be a wet week and keeping mud out would be a good thing.

Over time two others rolled in. Canadian Josh, a thirtysomething expat living in Singapore, and Dutchman Big Theo. Theodor, of Rotterdam in the Netherlands, once pedaled a bike all the way from his home in Western Europe across the entire Middle East. Standing around seven feet tall, the science behind his running movement must've made for next-level physics.

When we got to race weigh-in, my pack came in at nine kilograms (about twenty pounds), a full three kilograms (nearly seven pounds) lighter than the Namib. Much better.

We settled in and got horizontal to rest for the next day.

One thing different, one thing same.

It was a black banner this time—no electric green—that read in lowercase white letters running together: "racingtheplanet 2022." There was no chute this time, no corral. Perhaps it was easier to punch stakes in the desert than in the rocky Georgian soil. There was a line of national flags on either side of the start line. The only clue we were in Georgia was the white-and-red Georgian national flag, with a large red central cross and four smaller red crosses in each of its four white corners.

It was foggy again, like the first stage in the Namib. This time, though, the fog looked like it would hang around. In the Namib you knew the farther inland you ran, the fog would fade away. Not here.

It drizzled as Mary Gadams, owner and CEO of RacingThePlanet and the 4 Deserts series, talked us through the last few minutes to start for this twenty-five-mile stage. John was next to me as usual. We bumped fists and looked after the little things you look after when you're anxious but don't want to appear so. For me it was rubbing that little blue fabric square pinned to my chest pack.

I had a strange feeling on the start line. I was torn. My gear was great compared to last time. But given the short and eventful recovery—because Namib was only five weeks ago and life had pulled me in so many different emotions and directions since—I just didn't know how this would go. I had barely run since the Namib, so this felt like a trust fall where I truly didn't know what would happen, which left me with a scary thought.

At this point, I'm running less on training and more on faith.

I looked up to see Mary lift her arm, fire the pistol, and then—we were off!

I kicked out with the lead pack through the drizzle, at a nine-minute-per-mile pace. After about an hour, things were going well, but that fog got thicker and thicker until it was thicker than London's thickest.

I noticed a couple guys stopped ahead—Florian from Switzerland and Jeff from Canada. Jeff finished fourth in the Namib the year before and was a really experienced trail runner.

"Seen any pin flags?" yelled Jeff as I jogged closer.

"Not for a while. Too long," I said, as I stopped an arm's length away.

We realized now that we were off course. This was bad.

We decided to work together to fan out and see what we could, while we stayed close enough to maintain contact. We were there to beat one another, but the fog warranted a temporary truce. We scanned in the direction we thought the course might go but saw nothing. The pin flags were bright pink and should have been visible even through the whiteout.

Minute by minute, more guys arrived. Nobody could find the pin flags. We doubled back, and more and more runners bunched with us until we had eleven total in our pack.

The drizzle got colder. It was high thirties Fahrenheit, maybe low forties, classic hypothermia weather. We were all in spandex and light clothing. As our near-freezing, near-dozen group huddled and moved together, ten minutes passed, then twenty, then thirty.

After forty mostly stationary minutes searching, many of us had to pull off our race packs and pull on long sleeves and rain jackets.

We called the emergency phone number the race organizers provided. As out there as this race was, just in case someone had a phone with an international signal, the race gave us an "oh crap" local number to call. We called, gave coordinates to our location, and just as we did, a couple race staff ran up—the guys that marked the course in the first place.

"Hey, guys, you know where we're supposed to go next?" one of our pack yelled.

"Whoa, yeah, we don't know what happened. It's impossible to see, but I think I can get us over to where you should've turned," said the course marshal.

All of us followed him with eyes hungry for the next pink pin flag. As we walked through the fog, the course marshal said, "I don't see how this could have happened; we put extra flags out and checked them all last night. The farmer must have taken them or a cow stepped on and pulled them out or something. This doesn't make any sense."

"I see one!" someone yelled.

Suddenly everyone was pointing and cheering and pulling off rain gear. Mori Mori desperately ripped his rain pants down while on the run, one leg off, then hopped until he could yank the second pant leg clear of his other foot.

Everyone was in a mad dash for that first flag. Me too, and when I actually saw it, I got giddy.

I saw Florian and Jeff ahead of me, but other than that, I lost sight of everyone else in the scramble. It was pure chaos, except for the brief moment when I turned and saw Hiroki behind me on a hillside. Everyone just disappeared onto the course. The rain subsided and I came into Checkpoint 1, where Mary herself was under the rain cover.

"How are you, Matt?" she asked.

"Okay, but the fog is terrible," I responded, a little taken aback at the CEO checking in on me. I wondered if it was for me personally—like Sam checking in on me in the Namib, and perhaps they were worried about my kidney again—but that thought fell aside quickly. It was the fog. Not me.

"Good, we're working on the course mistake; I don't know what it was, but we'll find out. Just know you're on track and you're back on course and doing well."

I took that as a good sign and got on with my run. The rain and fog still made it hard to see, but I was extra careful to hit every pink pin flag and not miss another. I could not do that again.

Typical muddy terrain in Georgia.

Weaving my way uphill through the trees in Georgia.

I ran alone for the next few hours, and nearly twenty-eight miles later passed back under the black banner in the early afternoon. I hadn't seen anyone all day since our time lost in the fog together. I thought, *Maybe I'm the last one out on course. Maybe that's why I've been alone all day.*

But when I crossed the finish line, they weren't even banging the drums. There was nobody there. It was a ghost town. There was one person to check me off at the finish, but then I walked to tent #7, "Lake Bureti," and nobody was in. Not even Mori Mori. He beat me by an hour every day in the Namib. *Where is he? Why isn't he here?*

I took my stuff off and tried to dry off, and only twenty minutes after I finished did I get my first sighting of Florian and Jeff. They had finished first and second, respectively. Apparently Jeff only got me by a few minutes but ducked into his tent so quickly I didn't see him. I was a little in shock and again wondered, *Where's Mori Mori?*

The fog lifted but the sky stayed dark, threatening more rain. I looked toward the black banner and finish line and thought, *How long will they take?*

I had been out on course for around six hours, but my time, when they deducted a standard amount to allow for the course problem, came out to about four and a half hours.

The rest of the runners weren't so lucky. One by one they came in, all with horror stories about getting lost in the fog. Most runners had experiences worse than mine. Many didn't come in for hours and hours.

John came across the finish furious. Biblical anger. He marched through the finish line with a frozen scowl, straight to sit on a stool, muttering about how pissed off he was at how bad it all was. He wasn't wrong.

He'd organized a group that included the seventy-nine-year-old South Korean and stayed to keep that gentleman safe through the cold.[18]

---

18 Unfortunately, that older gentleman pulled out due to the hypothermic conditions.

John passed on coordinates to the race but the back-and-forth was garbled and the response too late. John had to get his group moving because the cold was getting dangerous. It was awful, and he bore the brunt of it.

I met him at the finish line, but his face was so angry I didn't get too close.

"Look, man, do what you've got to do to rest up and whatever you need—anything—just tell me what you need," I told him as he stomped to his tent. Over his shoulder, he said, "Just keep me in check if I need it."

I took his warning seriously enough to go straight to Zeana, the race's director, an American living in Thailand, who operated as second-in-command to Mary.

"As you can see, John's really angry right now and might just say something he'll regret. If you need someone to be a buffer, a go-between, please let me do that," I told her.

Zeana nodded.

I walked back to camp and kept an eye on John from a distance. He cooled off, slowly, over the next few hours.

Just as slowly, runners trickled into camp.

Everyone huddled extra close to the campfire to dry off and swap stories about the day. Ahmed took his insoles out of his shoes and put them next to the firepit's metal edge, but he left them there too long. The heat shriveled them down to half size, rendering them unusable.

I looked over and saw John eating his dinner, not scowling much anymore, and so I walked up and rubbed his shoulders.[19]

But I didn't have anything to say to make anything from that world's shittiest day any better. So I took a page from my parenting playbook. When all else fails, give them a hug. Or a shoulder rub. When you wear a pack all day, gravity pounds those muscles to mince. So I gave John what I would charitably call a B- shoulder rub.

---

19 What happens in Georgia stays in Georgia, I always say.

"Shoulder rubs?" came a sharply accented voice from Julie of Scotland. She was sitting next to John. Then everyone around the firepit raised their hands too.

"Okay, okay, just Julie and then I'm out!" I grinned, stepped laterally behind Julie, and started working on her. I made eye contact with John. We nodded.

I sat down to my own dinner. My watch told me I had burned 3,700 calories during today's run. Dinner consisted of a 510-calorie dehydrated mac and cheese and a handful of almonds.

I was frozen and nothing was dry, absolutely nothing. But it was a pretty good start nonetheless.

Who needs sleep anyway?

My überlight, überexpensive air mattress busted overnight. It didn't pop or puncture. Those I could fix with a patch kit. The internal cell structure failed, one by one, until it bubbled up so severely toward the head end that it put me in a fully upright seated position.

The ground was rocky. I guessed I'd be sleeping on it this week. Or not sleeping.

I was under the black banner an hour later than initially scheduled. The race gave us more time to rest because so many runners came in so late the day before.

I was wet. Drying off was pointless. If successful, I might be a little more comfortable to start the day. But one glance at the course—"Tsalka Reservoir"—showed a river crossing in the first mile and several more the rest of the day. I resigned myself to being wet. Even my daughters' blue blanky square was damp.

Crack!, the starter's pistol popped to begin the twenty-nine-mile stage.

I started the day fast, in and out of the river.

Running a river in Georgia.

Then, mercifully, we ran on a dry road for a while. I hung back in sixth until Checkpoint 1. Today's stage was long, so there wasn't a rush. Then one after another, I picked off the guys ahead of me until I climbed into third place.

We ran through several villages. They were neat, but the problem with the villages was that the only roads were made of dirt, which meant with all the rain they were now pure mud. It caked up onto our shoes, our legs, our ears.

We passed through a rural farming village where wild dogs roamed everywhere. The course marshals ran ahead of the runners to remind the locals to keep their dogs penned up. Over the day, though, I encountered at least two dozen, mostly Anatolian sheepdog–looking mutts, likely the products of big wolves and little bears.

In the village, a couple dogs were mean and got really close. An old Georgian farmer shooed them off with some choice words.

That was close, I thought.

Then even closer.

With two miles until the finish, I was running a long uphill climb on a ridgeline's dirt road spine. I saw Jeff up in the distance, maybe a half mile ahead. It was windy, really windy.

A pack of eight dogs ran toward him.

"Jeff! Dogs!" I yelled. "Jeff! Dogs!" But the wind was so loud there was no way he could hear me. Still, I kept at it. Over and again. He couldn't see what was coming at him, and I could see everything.

Then, finally, I saw Jeff turn to the dogs. They were on him.

He crouched down, gorilla-like, grabbed a rock, and faced them.

I was still running toward him. Yelling too. Because I thought maybe it would distract them and he could get clear, or maybe they'd be less likely to attack two of us. Or maybe I was running into a dogfight and I needed to psych myself up to throw down.

Jeff acted like he was going to hurl his rock at them. They halted. He did another throwing motion. They stayed. He did it a third time and slowly they turned away. Jeff pivoted and kept running.

I was up next. Now I was running toward a pack of dogs that just missed an opportunity. As I approached I grabbed my own handful of rocks. The dogs ran toward me and in seconds had me surrounded.

I slowed to a walk. They were feet from me.

Good grief, this is just like those fucking dogs in Iraq.

We saw the smoke on 9/11 because West Point isn't far north of New York City.

Through that fall and as the calendar turned over during the rest of our senior year, my cadet classmates and I wondered if we'd be sent overseas. President George W. Bush gave the commencement speech at our graduation on June 1, 2002, and his remarks included his assertion that we "be ready for preemptive action when necessary." We knew then we would go to war.

And we did. I spent the next several years either at war or preparing for combat. My unit, the Third Armored Cavalry Regiment, was in Iraq from the beginning and fought first in Fallujah and later, on another tour, became the counterinsurgency model for the "clear, hold, build" strategy in the northwestern city of Tal Afar.[20]

That first year was the hardest and harshest. In a few months I lost a commander I looked up to as the model of a great officer and gentleman (Captain Josh Byers); a soldier with so much life potential (Specialist Darius Jennings); and a classmate I'd sat next to in college courses and who I'd seen just days before he died (Lieutenant Todd Bryant). And then, for a moment, due to a mistaken message, I even thought my younger brother Rob had been killed fighting in another part of Iraq. When I got home, it all became a weight I couldn't push off.

So I started to run. My hockey-broken legs healed enough to handle some miles, and so on my second yearlong deployment, I'd jog on a treadmill in an old Iraqi air base hangar. I eventually graduated to the fresh, hot air, and even out to the camp's perimeter fence line. It was exactly two miles long by four miles wide, and dusty, so dusty, with so much sand. Physical challenge became my emotional respite.

Once, a pack of wild dogs got under the fence. It's inaccurate to call them "dogs," because those "dogs" were scarier than wolves. That particular day, seven of them slipped under the fence. I was out for a run on the perimeter by myself.

I stopped. I froze.

I turned my gaze away from them to demonstrate I wasn't a threat. For a good ten or fifteen seconds we stood there. They barked from five or six feet away but didn't get closer and didn't back away. I thought, *I've*

---

20 See George Packer, "The Lessons of Tal Afar," *New Yorker* (April 10, 2006).

made it through two years in combat and now I'm going to get eaten by wild dogs INSIDE the perimeter. WTF?

I caught a break. A few hundred meters away, beyond my field of view, one of the tower guards fired a couple warning shots beyond the fence, enough to scare them off. I ran straight back to the barracks, spine tingling the whole way.

I ran the same route the next day. No dogs.

I was not so lucky in Georgia. I looked away from them, just as I'd done in Iraq, thinking maybe I'd skirt by again.

I kept walking and thought in rapid-fire bursts: *Walk walk walk, just walk, keep walking, they won't do anything.*

At this point they fully surrounded me. I felt one open its mouth and nudge my hip, then a wet nose on my side, drool on my leg. Another did the same.

I kept walking and somehow, one at a time, the dogs peeled off and left me alone.

I picked my pace back up, finished the last couple miles—looking over my shoulder every few seconds—and came into a beautiful, treeless, high mountain camp in a boulder field. I pocketed a lesson from Jeff: Speak loudly and carry a big rock.

I finished third. Even better, I didn't see Mori Mori come in for over an hour. Yesterday wasn't a fluke; I was beating him. Really beating him. For a moment it was like someone had injected me with Superman's spit. I was feeling *up*, which was great but didn't last all that long because eventually my thoughts came back to Earth, back to Georgia, back to camp—where I had to go get hot water to rehydrate my dinner in a bag and then find a way to fall asleep in another bag on the rocky ground. Reality rapidly grounded my celebratory mood.

It was so windy we couldn't have a fire. There was a bright side to the wind, though. It pushed a cloud aside enough for the sunshine to peek through, officially the first time we'd seen the sun since leaving Tbilisi.

Black banner. Same drill. Twenty-four miles today.

If you were wondering, "mah-do-lo-ba" is how you say "thank you" in Georgian. That's what I was feeling at the third start line. A whole lot of mah-do-lo-ba.

I learned the expression from the Georgians who worked the race, keeping the hot water hot, keeping the tents tied down in the wind, and keeping the toilet pits clean(ish) in all the rain. They were phenomenal. They all had dark hair and the look of recently graduated high school wrestlers. They were goons, but good goons, which is why I liked them a lot.

They saved me some dry, heavy cardboard I could put under my sleeping bag. Despite the hard ground, the cardboard wasn't so bad. I got some sleep. I asked the good goon squad's leader how to thank them. He taught me my new favorite (and only) phrase in Georgian. I told him "mah-do-lo-ba." He fist bumped me, which is what good goons do.

I was halfway rested at the start line, ready to face a ferocious day. The conditions were windier, rainier, and rougher than we'd seen in the first two stages. But I was broken in to it. I just expected the sky to shit on me. It was now normal.

The runners exhibited several different approaches to the weather at the start line. Some just said, "Screw it," and wore regular running gear. Others went full on, looked as if they'd emptied their entire bag's worth of wet-weather items, and adopted an athletic hazmat suit aesthetic. I threaded the needle between the two. I wore my usual run stuff but pulled my poncho out and over my pack. It was optimistic in that I figured I could use it to stay dry but then pull it off easily should the rain subside.

Can't we catch a break? I thought as I rubbed my blue square, the pistol fired, and off we went.

As if a direct response to my appeal, somehow, as the first mile ticked by, the clouds cleared and a blue sky emerged. *Heaven!*

I ripped off my poncho and stuffed it in the side slot of my pack as I ran with Jeff. We were on a long dirt road for several miles along Tabatskuri Lake.

It was beautiful. A large, long climb from about 4,500 feet up to 7,500 and then back down to 6,000. We passed a lot of cows, goats, sheep, and, of course, dogs. Lots of dogs. Sometimes it felt like you couldn't walk fifty feet without bumping into mud, a cow pie, or a wild dog. (And sometimes you hit the trifecta—a muddy wild dog standing on a cow pie.)

Beyond the lake, most of today was on the old Silk Road. On arrival, I read that the original Silk Road ran through Baghdad, but wars and fighting forced a reroute through Georgia.[21]

Jeff broke ahead in the last mile and finished a little over a minute up on me for the day. We finished near Bezhano, a small village in a mountain bowl with green peaks in every direction. A stream separated our camp from the village, and a white-bodied stork with black-tipped wings wider than a basketball center's wingspan swooped over us.

I hit a runner's high that day. I felt good. Two in a row.

Camp life was awesome. It was more human (and grosser) than normal life. Everybody spent the afternoon talking. I met so many expats—a Scot living in Dubai, a Welshman in Japan, a Zambian in Norway. Even when the weather went wrong, the cross-country communication continued, just in smaller groups in our tents.

---

21 The United Nations now recognizes Georgia as a historical Silk Road country.

Camp conversation in Georgia.

We ate everything we could to stay upright. All that food going in meant it had to come out.

Whereas in the Namib we used porta johns, this time it was field latrines. Imagine you were in a drone hovering above our latrines (nobody's in there, don't worry, just stay with me). From above, you would see a boxy, number 9–shaped contraption made of tent fabric. The user entered from the open part of the 9, turned left, and then left again. After entry, there was a rope you affixed across the entrance to signify "in use." The user, now fully concealed from others, looked down to see an eighteen-inch-by-eighteen-inch square pit dug three feet deep. There were wood planks on either side of the pit to provide traction and stability for the job to be done.

I spent decades in the Army, so I've got a track record here.

Just after getting to Iraq, my cavalry squadron was in a temporary halt west of Baghdad. Nothing out there but dust and sand. To use the "bathroom" we walked out to the far side of a semitruck-sized transport vehicle that provided a barrier so the other guys couldn't see you.

One day I had to go suddenly, and I grabbed my commander's toilet stool, which is basically a couple pieces of aluminum that formed an X structure with a plastic seat fixed atop. You put a plastic bag underneath to catch your leavings.

I went around the giant truck and did as you do, but as I did, my commander was engaged in a conversation with, of all people, an attractive Australian journalist. I thought they were going to be there for maybe an hour, but apparently my commander was not a very good interviewee. Suddenly I heard the ignition on the journalist's civilian vehicle, and I realized, to my horror, that they were about to drive right in front of me as I made my grumpy.

So I did what any normal human being would do. I hurried. The aluminum legs on the toilet seat shifted in the sand. I fell off balance, plunged into my own poop.

Not a little. We had been eating MREs (meals ready to eat), so it had built up thick, and it was a lot. It covered the inside of my legs, all up and down, ankles to thighs.

There I was, lying in the sand, next to a road, coated in my own poop, pants still around my ankles, and a pretty Australian journalist was about to drive past me and likely put me on the cover of *Down Under* magazine to demonstrate a particularly low point in American foreign policy.

Some higher power intervened, and she stayed longer. So the worst never happened. But as I lay there, before I could clean myself up, I started to laugh out loud because I don't think you could design a situation in which you could feel more pathetic and exposed.

I expended an entire hundred-pack of baby wipes to clean myself off.[22]

---

22 This is why, by the way, many years later, I thought wet wipes would be a necessity in the Namib. But I digress.

One problem—the underside of the toilet seat was still packed with brown matter. I had borrowed it from my commander, so I knelt down, picked up handfuls of sand, then packed sand in to camouflage the evidence of my dirty deed, and then I tucked the seat and its now sand-coated underside back into my commander's Humvee.

The next day I woke up early to my commander yelling, "Davis! Davis!" (his soldier-driver).

"Davis, what the hell did you do to my toilet seat?"

I stayed silent, which, by the way, is what you do in such a situation.

———

So I've crapped in a lot of awful conditions.

Georgia was the worst. By a lot.

The rain filled those pits until the rising tide lifted all turds. It was absurd. Horrifying. And as if it couldn't get any worse, of course it did. When not running we all wore sandals with exposed feet, which meant our bare feet were poop-pit adjacent while in the very act of pooping. At one point the tip of my toe touched that which shouldn't be touched. And I did not care, not at all.

I'd like to think my time in the Army gave me an advantage here. But nasty is nasty.

———

I was under the black banner again for Stage 4's twenty-four miles. It felt like *Groundhog Day* but with sweat stains and muscle strains. I tapped the blue, then tucked it under some transparent plastic casing on my chest pack to keep it from getting wet. Because everything was going to get wet. Again.

Last night camp was assaulted by heavy rain and big hail, the kind that breaks car windshields. When the storm came, we retreated to our tents. So rest came early but loudly.

When we heard the *crack!* of the starter's pistol, a lot of us mistook it for lightning. The sky was still dark.

We took off and got five miles in without lightning. I was ahead of Jeff. When the lightning came, it came hard, and when I saw it hit the ground nearby I stopped to get my rain jacket on. It was a pain in the backside because it was back in the pack, so I had to take everything off just to get one thing on. But it was not a choice. It was a necessity.

As I got everything situated, Jeff ran up through the downpour.

"Stopped to get my rain jacket on," I said.

"Yeah," Jeff said.

"I think this is going to be sustained," I replied.

"Yeah, I think so too. How you doing? You're looking good, man, you went out pretty fast," said Jeff.

"Yeah, I feel pretty good."[23]

Jeff and I stayed together through several Georgian villages, including one where archaeological excavations have found evidence of Bronze Age settlements, weapons, and working tools. The people in these villages were poor. Not much appeared to have changed, beyond mobile phones, since the Bronze Age. Most looked to be subsistence farmers. Some stared at us in our spandex and sunglasses like we were aliens on Main Street.

Until mile twenty, Georgia giveth.

---

23 Not bloody Shakespeare, was it? I have video of this moment because Jeff was recording, so I know it's verbatim down to the syllable. But also, look, the rain was coming in sheets, and the hail was coming in hard, lightning too—and there was nowhere to hide in the open Georgian countryside. So our conversation was more for function and less for fun.

After mile twenty, Georgia taketh away.

Jeff and I hit a little uphill stretch, no big deal, right before a long downhill. Just then it was like someone tightened the screws in my right knee so much I couldn't flex to run. While the day before I had knocked out eight-minute miles on the downhills, now I could barely tolerate twelve-minute miles. Something was wrong.

The knee thing was somewhat expected and yet still troubling. Expected in that you can't run a hundred-plus miles in four days with a twenty-pound pack and not expect problems. But troubling too in that it was one of my two wheels, and I couldn't exactly bolt a spare on. You run on the wheels you've got.

Jeff moved ahead of me, finished ahead of me, and doubled back to check on me for the last few hundred meters.

"My right knee locked up," I explained.

"Ahhh, I thought so; I thought something happened," Jeff replied, then commanded, "Left here, left here! I missed it . . . walk it if you have to. Don't fuck up your knee!"

I turned in to the last couple hundred meters, feet coated in mud, appreciating that someone had my back out here, but I dwelled on his last words—*don't fuck up your knee.*

After the finish I headed straight to the medics. One gave me some Voltaren gel, a painkiller that you goop onto your skin to relieve the knee pain. I knew exactly what the diagnosis was because I'd had it before in my left knee. It was my IT band,[24] the band of tissue that runs all the way down from the hip through the kneecap.

I rested and gently stretched it, but I knew I was running on a wheel that was one loose nut away from falling off. I had no idea how tomorrow would go.

It's been a great week, I thought, *but sometimes great weeks come to*

---

24 Iliotibial band.

crashing ends. I was trying not to think what I was thinking, but I was thinking it all the same.

I just wanted to get to the end.

The race took pity on us, and we stayed the night in an emptied-out Soviet-era school, full of peeling lead paint and asbestos. It featured a ridiculously precarious floor-pit toilet where the concrete was ready to give way at any moment for the nastiest game of Russian roulette ever played.

Yet the school had one redeeming quality: It was dry.

We set out sleeping bags side by side in a few big classrooms. So instead of our more limited tent groups, we got to know some others. I chatted with Jeff, but also Mauricio of Mexico. Mauricio had come in behind me in fourth place every day, a total of ninety-five minutes back at this point, so we hadn't seen much of one another on the course. He was living as an expat in the restaurant business in Barcelona, and we talked about that. He asked how I was doing. So I just went out with it and told him about my IT band.

"I got you," said Mauricio, held up a pointer finger, turned, and walked over to reach for something in his race pack.

"Here, just get it back to me when you're done," he said, and he produced a small ball and foam roller, both solid, lightweight, made by Blackroll.

There was little to be done about a tight IT band, but what little that could be done required these exact two tools. The guy that was trying to catch me in this race just handed me the help I needed to stay ahead. His radical sense of generosity floored me. I thanked him and got to work to see what I could do to loosen the overtight screws in my right leg.

While rolling the IT band out, I thought about the general I worked for who was fond of saying, "Butter dudn't sharpen up steel," a good-ole-boy version of the expression "iron sharpens iron." He would use it to suggest we needed to toughen up training to toughen up troops.

But I could see it differently. From one view, Mauricio handing me this ball and roller might be a mistake that helped strengthen an adversary. I could also see the other view, and I thought Mauricio did too. The stronger your adversary, the stronger you become.

And so with Jeff too. Subconsciously and maybe consciously, I was sure he knew that if I was nipping at his heels he would have to run faster.

Our lives are shaped far more by gravity, our opposing forces, than we realize. If you want to run a certain speed, you have to find someone that runs that pace and then outrun them.

If they're at their best, you'll have to be at yours. Iron sharpens iron.

Before I closed my eyes, I said a little prayer for The Long March.

When I opened them, my prayer was answered.

Mary informed us she had cut the course from nearly fifty to about forty miles. Two reasons: There was a 100 percent chance of lightning and a 100 percent certainty we would encounter several dozen wild dogs at the Abuli Fortress ruin on the original course. Cutting Abuli Fortress out was both safer and a little shorter.

This was good for me. My ninety-five-minute cushion on Mauricio meant I had room to give. I was nervous but feeling game as I stood under the black banner, rubbed my blue square, and then stepped off for The Long March.

I started fast and fine. I came into the halfway mark, around mile twenty, sitting in my usual third place, back from Florian and Jeff by about ten minutes. I hit the Coke jackpot at a checkpoint and loved every sip.

A quick checkpoint stop in Georgia.

Not long after was when I felt it. My IT band tightened at precisely the same mile mark as yesterday. I was on a long stretch of grassy, sloping, uneven terrain. I couldn't see anybody in any direction.

First things first, I panicked. I mean, I really panicked. I yelled for someone to help. There was nobody. I yelled into a black hole.

When I calmed myself down, realized there really was nobody but me, I stopped and pushed on the IT band. I walked. I massaged it. I stretched while walking. I stopped to stretch.

I did the mental math.

My leg's fucked, and I'll need it for the Atacama in a couple months. Mauricio's likely pushing twelve minutes a mile today. Let's say he does that the rest of the day. Worst case he passes me in a few minutes. If I can hold a hard walk at fifteen minutes per mile, that means Mauricio would gain three minutes every mile for at most twenty miles. Worst case he can cut sixty minutes into my overall ninety-five-minute lead, but then there's no way he can make up thirty-five minutes on the final short stage.

To preserve my leg and my lead, I power walked the rest of the way. I'd never walked in a race like this. And to do it for twenty miles, at four miles per hour, meant I had to feel like the walking dead for five full hours.

I walked and thought. About Kevin.

"You saved my life," read the handwritten card Kevin gave Rachel and me in 2013. I looked up, hugged him, and reminded him of how far he had come through his own hard work. Later that night, Rachel and I, in the quiet of our bedroom, acknowledged how stunned we were.

Before I met Rachel I had promised my younger brother Kevin he could live with me. He weighed nearly 350 pounds at the time, and I offered to support him in order to exercise and lose weight so he could pursue his wish to join the military.

Which meant, when we met and dated, I had to tell Rachel that my little brother Kevin would also reside in our first home together in 2009. (She took this news far better than most and became one of his greatest supporters.)

It was difficult at first. We lived in a small townhouse with a little basement apartment. Kevin slept on a tiny built-in twin bed that he extended over like an oversized manhole cover. The shower was too small for me, and I can only imagine how he did it. However, three blocks away there was a great new gym and he set to work. Kevin went to spin classes. He spent hours and hours on treadmills and elliptical machines. He walked—a lot.

It worked. Under a year later, Kevin weighed 225 pounds. It felt like a miracle.

But when he moved back to Minnesota, the weight came back quickly to about 255 pounds in just months. He stabilized just below that peak after that, but not long after, a deadline came into view. Because he had to sign up with the military by his twenty-seventh birthday, Kevin would have to lose over sixty-five pounds in only three months.

In the meantime, in 2011, Rachel and I had moved to Wellington, New Zealand, and were closing in on Grace's birth.

Because this was so important to Kevin, I asked Rachel if he could—again—stay with us for two more months in New Zealand to make a final push before the deadline. She was hesitant. If he came, he would be with us in our small home for the seventh and eighth months of her first pregnancy. This was the toughest stress on our young marriage.

Ultimately, she agreed to it, and he did fly down and move in—though with several caveats, and we moved him over to a hostel for the last few weeks. But it worked again. In fifty-eight days Kevin lost over sixty-five pounds and got to 187 pounds. He signed with the Army.

A couple years later, while serving in the Army, he broke his foot. The weight came back.

I felt awful because I couldn't help again. I felt like I'd fallen short, like I couldn't keep the one brotherly imperative I knew to follow—I am my brother's keeper. Maybe in some rational part of my mind I knew I couldn't do everything for everyone, but not succeeding at helping my own brother left a mark nonetheless.

The long walk hurt my pride.

Somehow I had enough of a lead that Mauricio didn't pass me until mile twenty-nine.

Late in the day, I walked through a village where the kids came out. A little gang of three-, four-, and five-year-olds made a game of running past me as if we were racing. One blew past me, then pretended to be old and slow, all while his little buddies laughed. Nothing, I mean nothing, makes you feel smaller than a toddler who demonstrates actual physical superiority over you. It was humiliating and hilarious all at once.

When I crossed the finish line, my rough estimate bore out. I lost thirty-six minutes to Mauricio on The Long March. With that ninety-five-minute buffer to start the day, I was still in third overall by a solid margin.

I woke the next cold morning to a crisis. I was nearly out of toilet paper. My tiny dehydrated tablets were out, so I had to bum a couple from John.[25] Luckily the good goons left some TP in the latrines for common use, and I did the one ungentlemanly thing you shouldn't do—I unspooled as much extra as I could stuff in my pockets for myself. Selfish, I know.

Even then I ran out, again, despite rationing myself to 1.5 squares per "use." Just when I ran completely out, Big Theo came through with a little of what he had left. And when a guy that size shares what little TP he has left—well, his kindness matched his size.

Unlike the Namib, on the post–Long March down day, I still had some food to tide me over. I held on to a 1,000-calorie porridge with strawberries that was excellent. And at 5 PM, the race brought us all a special treat—tomatoes, cucumbers, and bread from the local village. I ripped right into the fresh tomatoes and bread until seeds and crumbs coated my cheeks. My good goon fairies came through yet again. *Mah-do-lo-ba*, goons, *mah-do-lo-ba*.

Today the mystery finally revealed itself. I learned why Mori Mori had such a hard time that week. I had seen him cough because I had given him cough drops from my bag all week. But that day I walked in the tent as Hiroki taught Mori Mori the English word for "diarrhea," which, by

25 "Bum" pun intended and earned.

the way, is a really funny word to watch someone sort out proper pronunciation for. And just when funny was in short supply.

Everyone was dinged up. John hurt his knee two-thirds of the way through The Long March, as he put it, running past a "shifty farm with some mean-ass dogs."

We woke to a clear-sky morning, with a perfect view across a canyon to Vardzia, a twelfth-century fortress with hundreds of rooms, our destination for the last few miles of the week.

We started at the top of a ridgeline on one side of the canyon. I looked down into an enormous gorge as I touched my blue square for the final time this week, and I heard the final gun go off. It was a simple proposition—six miles of downhill switchbacks to the finish.

I found myself standing next to Mauricio and ran with him. We both had IT band pain. A mile or so in, I realized how awful it was to limp the last few miles in silence. I blurted out, "Best Mexican actor of all time?"

Mauricio seemed like he didn't know what to make of what I had just said. I doubled down and suggested, "Javier Bardem." As soon as it left my mouth, I said, "My bad, my bad, he's Spanish I think." By now Mauricio hadn't responded. I was worried I sounded like a jerky gringo.

But then he chimed in with some thoughts, and we opened up some great back-and-forth. He told me more about his business in Barcelona, his life in transit from Mexico to college at Cornell to work in Boston and then on to Spain.

As we came into the finish, he said he appreciated the conversation, that it took his mind off his pain. To me that felt like two finishes instead of one.

To cross that finish line was a relief—I came in third place overall—and to nail it down at a place that was a thousand years old. We toured the ancient Vardzia complex, and while walking the grounds I realized something.

I don't have to be so lonely. Yeah, it's lonely to be separated from my family. But it helps to be with my tribe by choice.

Accepting my third place award in Georgia, with Josh and Elise in the image at left.

Call it campfire magic. Because these events were held so far from where runners typically roam, there were no homers here. Everyone was at an away game. Everyone arrived eyes wide open. Nothing was familiar.

When you were at the campfire, the English was so-so, but the conversation was stupendous. Because the campfire was the only entertainment there was all week. It provided warmth. It provided light. But it also provided warm and enlightening conversation, a tractor-beam pull that got you out of your tent and into a circle with fellow runners. Maybe that appealed most: We were all equal in the circle. So we talked about our day's run as equals, without regard for who went faster or who walked or who struggled. We were all sitting there, hungry, cold, and appreciating that we could have a little community-made entertainment.

It was here I realized I likely had more in common with these people from two dozen other countries—Hong Kong, South Korea, and Zambia—than with my biological kin. We all looked up from our lives and jobs at various dots on the globe, heard about this very long race, and said, "Yeah, I want to do *that*."

When around that self-selected group, that tribe, you could feel it. Whatever that feeling was, it was the opposite of lonely. I needed that.

But what I felt in my mind was one thing. What my body was feeling was another. I was really bent up but at least not broken. There was another starting line to come in the Atacama Desert, the world's highest and driest, in eleven weeks.

ACTION THIS DAY

Your adversaries can be your truest friends. They push you to perform, they illuminate your strengths, they highlight your weaknesses. They can be the iron you sharpen yourself against.

Who does this for you now? Who might do this for you? How can you harness that dynamic for your own benefit (and even theirs)?

In Georgia I saw it, the same perfect blend of competition and cooperation. To compete means, in its Latin root, to "strive together." It is possible to compete and cooperate at the same time.

The world needs more, a lot more, events like this. Places where competitors are as fierce as they are civil. Where you'd be willing to help an opponent sometimes, because by doing so, you make yourself stronger, sharper, better.

Chapter Seven

YOU CAN'T SHOOT A CANNON FROM A CANOE

This is it. Last chance for a never-was.

July 14, 2022
Great Moves Physical Therapy
Colorado Springs, Colorado

"Aaaaaahhhhh! Ughhhhhh!"

I tried to hold it in, really I did, but the needle going into my groin a millimeter from my manhood went way past my pain point. The entire physical therapy practice could hear my shouts, maybe dogs in Kansas too.

Fernando, my therapist, already had five needles spread across my backside and hip, and he saved the sixth for the most sensitive spot. I was a human pincushion. He sent those dry needles into my butt, hip, and groin in an effort to engage the muscles as deep as possible to get them to uncoil and heal. It was torture. Sweat-inducing, cringing, seizing and shouting, white-knuckle pain.

But the progress we'd already made kept me coming back to that torture table. My IT band loosened a little every visit, and it took five more dry-needle sessions to get back to my normal running stride. He advised stretches as well, which I did in my little apartment.

My foundation had cracked like bad concrete. If I was going to make the Atacama I needed to fix it. I knew the hard way from bad sports experiences that fundamentals always come first. Growing up in Minnesota I was a skating stereotype, because like (nearly) all Minnesotans, I started playing hockey as soon as we could gather the gear. As I got older, strength training became part of the game. Back then the Ice Gods were the Golden Gophers college hockey players and coaches. I remember going to a hockey camp where one of the Gophers mentioned as an aside, "You can't shoot a cannon from a canoe." It was meant to nudge us to focus on leg strength as foundational for hockey.

They were right and not just about hockey. No base, no platform, no bedrock, and you've got nothing. I saw it in every military unit I ever served in. The ones that had one prospered. The ones that didn't suffered.

I know because I myself have lacked one before. I also know because I'm an athletic never-was.

I was always better at effort than success in sport. Coaches loved that I tried harder than almost everyone on my teams. And that got me somewhere.

I played everything once. Soccer, speed skating, golf, tennis, baseball, hockey, and I dabbled in skiing despite the distinct lack of mountains in Minnesota.

I broke everything once. Each of those sports, one by one, ground to a halt for injuries or some physical limitation. Tendinitis and bad eyes and broken bones and major surgeries. My body would fall apart at the worst moments.

Hockey, maybe by default, became my primary sport. I wanted to play in college more than anything. Money aside, it was the driving consideration in my decision to go to West Point. It was how I saw myself—even if the accolades and accomplishments were thin.

Still, it didn't pan out. While at West Point, I spent more time rehabbing in the trainer's room than I did on the ice. I broke bones in combatives class and had extensive orthopedic work on my left knee, which resulted in a procedure to remove one-third of the patellar tendon. I'd been told that the tendon had been frayed to such a degree that it would be better to simply remove a portion.[26]

When I left West Point, I couldn't run at all. I wasn't doing much of anything. I had a medical excusal not to run during unit physical training. As we got ready to deploy to Iraq for the first time, I asked our unit physician's assistant if it was a problem that I had this official lower-body limitation.

"Just don't run from the enemy, you'll be fine," he told me, deadpan as the deadest pan.

For years I lost my athletic self. I did nothing physical. The knee prevented it. It wasn't until my second tour in Iraq that running took off for me, out on that dusty perimeter fence line, and I rediscovered something I could compete in.[27]

That left me with a lingering feeling that I had business that needed a finish. And at that point in the Grand Slam—about to turn forty-three years old—I felt I hadn't yet peaked athletically.

So I would have taken a million needles, wherever they needed to go, into my eyeballs if necessary, to get ready for the next race. When Fernando finished, he left the room, I changed out of my then sweat-soaked clothes and drove home.

Sixty-nine days until departure for the Atacama.

---

26 I later learned that this procedure, at the time fairly common for athletes including baseball catchers (e.g., Iván "Pudge" Rodríguez), is now frowned upon. As I understand it, today's preferred treatment is nonsurgical.

27 Which was also when that official lower-body physical restriction was lifted.

Fernando's work was successful. By early August I progressed enough that I took on a three-day event as a training race, went back to my running origins at the TransRockies Run in Colorado. The TransRockies, like the 4 Deserts events, was a multiday race, which made it a good stepping stone for the Atacama. Rachel left the girls in Utah with family and we met at the race, where she had volunteered for so many years that she had come on board as paid staff. We finally had some time alone, even if it meant I had to run for it.

The TransRockies was a more humane version of the 4 Deserts, where they provided far more than just a tent and water. Of course the miles were tough—but the après run was dialed in to marshmallow-cush perfection.

The third stage at the TransRockies was the longest, and for those in the three-day event, it was our last day. The past couple days I had been near a runner named Mike. We had run on one another's heels so far—and I knew he would finish ahead of me—that I would still make the podium in second place, so we ran together the last ten miles or so to the finish in a pristine mountain valley at 9,200 feet—a location that would be formally named an American national monument just months later (Camp Hale-Continental Divide National Monument).[28] On the long dirt road approaching the stage's end, still kicking hard, Mike told me about the guy who got him into running trail races and how sad he was that person had passed away.

"Whenever I get close to a tough day's finish," Mike said, "I try, if I can, to think about him, and the others who made my running possible."

His final-mile-gratitude practice sunk in with me.

I had done the TransRockies so many times at this point (eight), and my natural interest in the local environment and towns meant that over time I had gravitated toward giving nightly talks about the local sights

28 See ML Cavanaugh, "Colorado gets a national monument to war's potential to make 'a better peace'," *Los Angeles Times* (Oct. 12, 2022).

and stories to help the many out-of-town runners better appreciate this part of Colorado's coolness.

That night, in front of several hundred runners, I told them about my kidney donation and my experiences in the Namib and Georgia, as well as my upcoming races in the Atacama and Antarctica. I ended with a simple point: "You can donate a kidney, you can save a life, and you can go right back to running or doing whatever it is that you love. I know because I have." While I had continued blogging on life after kidney donation and the races, so far, my advocacy felt like I'd been lobbing bottled messages into an ocean of apathy. Nobody cared. And really, should they have? If a guy donates a kidney and runs so far off the beaten path that nobody sees it, did it ever really happen?

That night, however, after I finished and walked out of the big tent, two women came over. The first was a woman whose father had passed away from a genetic condition that caused kidney failure. She had the same condition as him and told me that she was sure that she would someday need a transplant, but that nobody in her family would be eligible to donate because they all had the same genetic bad luck. She was a runner just like me, but through no fault of her own, she'd lost the kidney health lottery. She told me she was thankful that someone in the run community cared about her predicament.

The second woman who came up was another runner, someone I'd met informally before. She told me she was at a point in life that she would consider kidney donation. I gave her some contact information and hoped she'd keep at it.[29]

This moment, outside a tent in a beautiful valley in the Rocky Mountains, was my first real sense that the running advocacy had broken through. I knew then that I wasn't just running circles in deserts—that

---

29 She did keep at it. We stayed in contact as mentor-mentee all the way through her successful kidney donation the following year. She continues to live a full life and does challenging athletic events.

word was getting out, that runners and maybe others would consider kidney donation because they saw that they could and continue to live full, active lives.

Forty-nine days until departure for the Atacama.

I couldn't stop yawning. It was like my body was actively rebelling against my twenty-seventh and final training run of the month on Wednesday, August 31. Still, I got up and got out and got onto the pavement in the dark and got my twenty miles, which made 410 total for the month.

I was so excited I forgot to shave. I had to turn around halfway to work and go home to shave (that's how big a no-no it is to show up stubble-faced in the military).

But I didn't care. My physical self had healed. I was back on track for the Atacama.

Beyond running, it took so much work on the basics. Like hammer and tongs and blowtorch and ditch-digging work to force my foundation back to solid.

First, sleep. I had starved myself of a full night's rest for several years. My standard was about six hours. I needed to get that up to eight hours a night, so I went to bed at 8:30 PM and got up at 4:30 AM. Monastic, I know, but I think the monastic life was necessary for the improvement I needed.

Next, sauna. The last week before departing for the Namib I did what I could to train for the heat in a local sauna. Although "acclimation" may be an overstatement—the temperatures in the Namib Desert consistently topped 115 degrees, even far higher, and the sauna could only get up to 105—I think it helped at least a little. I did ultimately survive, so maybe that helped me get over the heat enough to make it to the finish line. I continued that practice for the Atacama—to put another brick in the foundation.

Another goal I worked toward was getting my pack down to six kilograms (a little over thirteen pounds). That was almost absurd to me considering I had started this all with double that weight in the Namib. But if I could cut three more kilograms off my back compared to Georgia, it would make a big speed difference.

How much more can I cut?

Twenty-one days until departure for the Atacama.

In September I had dinner with John and Karen Bezou at a local Mexican restaurant. It was decision time for John. His injury in Georgia was far worse than we'd thought. He'd dislocated a joint in his knee and had a tear in his meniscus, requiring platelet-rich plasma (PRP) injections.[30] While I was at the TransRockies, John traveled to northern Finland to try his luck on that wonky knee for the additional race in the Grand Slam.[31]

At dinner, John explained, "I hit the first big water crossing and it just wouldn't go. I had to pull out or risk the rest of the Slam."

He'd kept up the PRP injections but wasn't able to do any training, at all, for weeks. He had dreamed of this series for years and now it was all in jeopardy.

"We're almost a week out—are you going?" I asked John.

"I can't do what I want to do, and I've been on the fence," John said. "But there's no makeup. I gotta go."

He wasn't game ready, but John was a gamer. He knew he'd be far below 100 percent, but he wanted to be on the start line regardless.

I was relieved. I wouldn't know what to do without him. For me, he was as much a part of these things as the heat, sand, and my little blue square.

Eight days until departure for the Atacama.

---

30 They draw blood, separate out the plasma, and inject the platelet-rich plasma into the injured area to stimulate healing.

31 This was the "Plus" race.

I walked past the high school kid flexing in the gym's locker-room mirror, opened the sauna door, and sat with my thoughts for as long as I could handle the heat.

This is it. Last chance for a never-was.

Final sauna session before leaving. Thirty-five minutes. Plenty of time to think.

What if I could win this thing?

At the finish line in Georgia, one of the race officials told me I was now in the hunt for the 4 Deserts Champion trophy.

Here's how they figured. Remember, us Grand Slammers weren't competing against the runners that just did one-off races. We were in it for a longer haul.

I finished third in Georgia; Mori Mori finished sixth. Add in my fourth place at the Namib, and Mori Mori's second, that gave me a one-place edge on him—I now had a 7, he was at an 8.[32] And Michele was already behind with his two fifth places, which left him with 10. So among this year's Grand Slam men, I was in the lead.

Unfortunately for me, I also learned the 4 Deserts Champion award was separate from the Grand Slam. The Grand Slammers all aimed to do the races in a single calendar year or less. The 4 Deserts Champion, however, wasn't bound by chronology. It was crowned only in years when they ran The Last Desert in Antarctica (typically in even years), a race where all the competitors qualify to be there by having run at least two of the other races in the 4 Deserts series. What that meant was everyone in Antarctica would have a RacingThePlanet resume. The champion, then, was crowned by being the one with the lowest cumulative previous-finish total in the three other races.

---

32 Each place counts as one point (e.g., second = two points, fourth = four points, and so on). Lowest point total is best.

Which was how I was still behind. A German runner about my age, Ben Dame, would also compete in Antarctica. He'd had a second place from the Atacama Crossing in 2016, a third place from the Gobi March from 2017, and a second place from the Namib Race in 2021. Add those up, and his magic number was 7, same as mine.

But he had also finished ninth overall at the Namib Race in 2018 and then went back in 2021 to "replace" that result (with a second).[33] So that's how Grand Slammers got screwed in the standings. Others get multiple tries. Grand Slammers get one shot.

That's why I was behind. We had the same magic number, but I still had the Atacama Crossing to get through. This meant to win 4 Deserts Champion, I had to win the Atacama first. That would give me a first, which would bring my number to 8, only one point behind Dame. It would also hold off Mori Mori, so even if he finished second in the Atacama, he would be two points behind me with a 10.

That would set up a duel with Dame in Antarctica. Winner wins. I'd be so close he'd have to beat me, and I'd be close enough that if I won, I'd win. Head-to-head. A fair shot.

For me to finish second in Atacama, or even worse, third, would leave little opportunity in Antarctica.

So the only way forward was that first I had to win the Atacama. No small feat. The race would start at 10,500 feet, and if I was lucky, that's where we would race for the week. Living in Colorado, I could get up high and build a base that would be hard to beat.

But that's not how the race would go. It dropped after the first stage. The majority of the week would be at about 7,000 feet.

Then there would be the non–Grand Slam runners, the ones with fresher legs. The big dogs there would be the two runners who won the

---

33 Not to pile on here, but a more fair and reasonable policy might be to instead use an average of the two races. In this case, a ninth and second place at the Namib would equal 5.5 points. (Remember, motivated reasoning still counts as reasoning.)

last two Namib Races. 2021's Namib Race winner was Rob Ripley, who was a cancer survivor who had turned into an endurance monster. In addition to Rob, there would be Reinhold, the Swiss runner who beat me by several hours in the Namib a few months back. Of course that left out the unknown competition that might show.

Was this even possible? Or was I asking the universe for two impossibles in a row? To beat a bunch of guys who recently outran me? Then again, beat another guy who had achieved a higher place than me over several of the same races.

Do I have any other choice? How many more opportunities will I get like this? This one's a big deal. 4 Deserts Champion. Atacama. Antarctica. Titles worth the struggle.

I looked up and saw my sauna time was nearly done. I looked over to the edge of my shoulder, where, for several days now, I had marked a half dozen spots on my upper back, shoulders, and collarbone with a black permanent marker. When I would get in from a run, having trained with the pack I'd carry in the Atacama, I marked the red spots so I'd know where the pack would burn the skin. That way pre-race I could protect those places at least a little with tape.

It was a hard thing to know for certain that my back would again feel semiconstant slicing for yet another week. The thought of even more raw skin made me nauseous. That thought lingered while I packed my things from the sauna.

It led me to another thought: *I can't do this by myself. I need help.*

Finished, I opened the gym door, drove home, and when I got there I immediately reached for my laptop and fired off a last message to the social media universe for help:

> For anyone reading this—family, family-friends, close-friends, distant-friends, friends-I-have-yet-to-meet—I'd like to ask something of you.
>
> During race week, September 25th to October 1st, the organizers maintain a satellite-internet-enabled-computer, where the racers can

receive email from the wider world. Send me something, anything, a funny story about your day, about your kids, about your dogs, about how you're doing, about a person you know with a kidney-ailment . . . or even a really amazing dinner you just had. It can be anything you think might help me take my mind off the race for just a minute, and I can tell you, from experience, it will help.

Go to the race site and click "send an email." And whatever you type will travel thousands of miles south to me, at the very end of my very long day.

One day until departure for the Atacama.

ACTION THIS DAY

Everyone knows you can't shoot a cannon out of a canoe.

What's your foundation? How strong, how steady is it?

We should question the basics every so often. Just how solid are we, really? What are our load-bearing assumptions, and what would it take to knock them out?

Everyone has keystones—of the mind and in our lives—and it's good to check in once in a while to ensure they're reasonable and acceptable and acknowledged.

My gut tells me that when we look around and scrutinize our life, our work, and our relationships, our day-to-day is on thinner ice than we'd care to admit. What's your critical infrastructure? What support systems can't you lose?

Because if your cannon's cocked atop a canoe, you'd better think twice before you fire.

Chapter Eight

NOBODY SLAYS DRAGONS ALONE

RACE ACROSS THE DRIEST DESERT—THE ATACAMA

I crossed the Atacama Desert without someone beside me. But I was never alone.

September 22, 2022
Flight 152
Santiago to Calama, Chile

I'm going to a desert race in San Pedro," the young woman next to me on the flight said.

"Then I think we're headed to the same place—RacingThePlanet?" I asked.

"Yes, it's my first one." Her British accent was clear, even through her Covid mask.

After we wiped down our seats and tray tables and armrests with sanitizing cloths, we chatted for two hours about what to expect at the race. Her name was Gemma. Originally from the United Kingdom, she now worked as a nurse in Ohio. She exuded enthusiasm. I told her everything I could about what to expect as if I were a veteran. I supposed that, this being my third race in five months, maybe I had become somewhat experienced.

Talking made the flight pass quickly. We landed in Calama, a mining town in northern Chile, and boarded a rickety bus bound for San Pedro de Atacama, a ninety-minute drive to the southeast. We passed a road sign pointing to Tocopilla, made famous by mention in Johnny Cash's song "I've Been Everywhere."[34]

I really was racing *everywhere.*

San Pedro de Atacama grew up around an oasis. About 5,000 people permanently live there. The settlement predates the Incas and sits at around 8,000 feet elevation atop a plateau that occupies 70,000 square miles.

San Pedro is the gateway to the Atacama Desert, which is twenty million years old and at one point was under the sea. Roughly the size of Kentucky, the desert holds much of the world's copper and lithium reserves (lithium being a major component in electrical vehicle batteries). It is the driest desert in the world, and some weather stations in the Atacama have never recorded rain. The soil's been compared to Mars, and the dry air and low levels of artificial light from cities create exceptional conditions for seeing stars (the area is home to some of the largest telescopes in the world).

When we arrived in San Pedro, we found what looked to be an empty city. Everything was red or brown or reddish-brown—no green as far as the eye could see. The entire city looked like an enormous compound, surrounded by walls. When the bus entered the city streets, we found dusty roads with a small sidewalk on either side. There were no front yards, just

34 From Cash's album, *American II: Unchained* (1996), based on an Australian folk song by Geoff Mack.

buildings stacked together. Very few windows faced the street. Even what was supposed to be white had turned brown over time with thick coats of dust.

Every doorway provided a portal to another world—hotels, restaurants, pharmacies, or shops.

I found my hotel and rested up.

The next morning, after breakfast I walked down the dusty streets to a wooden door where John told me to meet him. He'd chosen a smaller hotel. His hotel's central courtyard was a little oasis. It must have had a water source somewhere I couldn't see, because there were little scrub trees and plants, some big enough to provide shade.

John agreed to help bandage my upper back and shoulders, and he even brought extra medical gear from his past life as a military medical service corps officer to patch me up.

I sat at a picnic table and looked around first. The coast was clear. I was hesitant to be doing something vaguely medical in an area that was clearly for relaxation in a hotel's central courtyard. When I was convinced nobody was watching, I took my shirt off.

John cleaned the scars and scabs with some scrub, then applied two rectangular padded bandages, each the size of large notecards, over the worst spots. Then he extended two long strips of black RockTape from my shoulder blades up over to the left of my neck and down over my collarbone. He repeated the same process on the right side. When I put my shirt back on, black tape crawled up toward both ears.

"How are *you* doing?" I asked, suspecting a grim answer.

"I'm good. I mean, this isn't what I wanted, but this is what I got. At least I can keep you pushing hard."

Beyond my question, John never once mentioned his knee injury, but I knew his torn meniscus was on his mind. He wanted to run but was resigned to a week of jogging and hard hiking. He took some real sour lemons and made lemonade. Selfishly, no matter what shape his knee was in, I was glad he was there.

We loaded our race packs and walked to pre-race check-in. The roads were fuller today with tourists, who kicked up clouds and coated our shoes in dust as we walked. We passed by a couple doors painted blue and turquoise, and the rest were mostly propped open to entice tourists with colorful shops.

When we arrived at gear check, it was like first sight of your friends on the other side of summer break. I spotted Julita first.

"Big woman!" she shouted down toward me, smiling, both pointer fingers turned in toward herself.

"Little man!" I responded back up, thumbs inward, grinning ear to ear, as I leaned in for a hug.

I took the pre-race Covid test and came out clean again.

Whew! Three for three, I thought.

Weigh-in went well: My pack was down to 7.5 kilograms (about 16.5 pounds), which put me on the lighter side. I'd cut nearly 40 percent from my pack weight since the Namib.

I finished weigh-in and looked over to spot Mori Mori chatting with another Japanese runner. I couldn't help but interject to welcome my always yellow-hatted, orange-shirted competition. I offered a giant smile and a hand, and we did the pull-in one-shoulder, lean-in half-hug guys do.

"Feel better?" I asked, wanting to know if he'd come back from that awful week in Georgia. Of course my concern had two parts—his well-being and what his well-being meant for my own race-week well-being.

He started a syllable in Japanese, then switched to English, using hand gestures to aid. He said, "After race—Covid."

Then he made a hands-folded, head-tilt motion to signify sleep. "Long time . . . then I can run." He literally started to jog to show me.

"So you feel good now?" I asked.

"Now, okay," he smiled.

Now I knew. It was on.

The next day we rode buses north into the Arcoiris ("Rainbow") Valley, pulled off the road, grabbed our packs, and stepped onto Chilean Mars, elevation 10,500 feet. Even the white tents the race and medical staff used looked stolen from NASA.

The runners' tents were still olive-drab green, military style, and formed two lines that pointed toward the start line. We were surrounded on three sides by hills and hoodoos, enormous surface stalagmites in chaotic clumps, all reaching for the clear blue sky. The "rainbow" of colors was a far narrower rainbow range than normal life but far greater than the rest of the Atacama. Reds and shades of red, tans and shades of tan, even little glimpses of muted greens and chalky whites were embedded in the rocks.

Relative to the rocky canyon, the start chute was a riot of colors, with the flags of thirty-nine countries leading toward a bright yellow banner with black bold lettering: "ATACAMA CROSSING 2022."

The start chute was fuller than it had ever been, not just in quantity but quality too. This was a really tough field. All the Grand Slammers were there. And, as anticipated, both recent Namib winners too: Reinhold and Rob were there. Gabriella, a one-armed Norwegian woman, had beaten drug addiction and was now ultrarunning as a shoe company–sponsored athlete. Vladmi, a blind runner from Brazil, had finished seven previous 4 Deserts events, typically at the middle of the pack despite not seeing a single dangerous step. Jack Jarvis, an ex–British Army soldier, had recently rowed 111 days solo across the Atlantic Ocean to set a Guinness World Record. The staff told us a longer-haired Brit, Rob—aka "Bilbo Baggins"—would run fiercely fast. And Jodi, an airline pilot from Alaska who donated a kidney in 2017 to save the life of a flight attendant she'd known, had since climbed Kilimanjaro, Aconcagua, and ridden her bike 1,200 miles through the desert from Tijuana to Cabo San Lucas.

And of course there was Mori Mori. I looked over to see him wearing his same yellow hat, his same orange shirt. There was one difference: His cheek bulged with something. I didn't think it was tobacco.[35] It must've been something else. *Maybe some kind of caffeine?*

I looked down to his race-assigned number on his front: #81.

Perfect, I thought. The race had given me #18. *My mirror image.*

I looked around, but John wasn't near me in the start chute. He knew his knee would be clunky and didn't want to get caught in the rush out the gate. If he were nearby, I might've asked him for a hug it was so cold.

I was freezing. We could see the sun off in the distance, but the high canyon walls prevented the rays from getting to us. So everyone in the chute shivered in sync with the party music the race blared. Most runners wore jackets and arm sleeves. I knew from past experience that I warm up quickly, so I was just in my shirt and shorts. My two nods to the cold were my thin black gloves and my neck gaiter pulled up over my face. I looked like an athletic bandit.

Although CEO Mary Gadams was there, Sam Fanshawe was back as race director. I hadn't seen her since the Namib, and she was a friendly face. No pistol this time. She got on a loudspeaker and started counting down.

"10, 9, 8, 7, 6 . . ." For the thirteenth time at a RacingThePlanet start line this year I touched my blue square for good luck ahead of our twenty-two-mile stage.

Sam continued in Spanish, "cinco, cuatro, tres, dos, uno, GO!"

We took off into a narrow down-sloping channel, past a red earthen exclamation point shooting straight out of the ground. I let some guys go ahead because the footing was loose rocks, and I didn't feel like fighting yet. It was too cold. I needed to warm up first.

---

35 That would've been against Minnesota State High School League rules, don'tcha know.

I ran near the yellow hat for much of the day. Mori Mori was just behind me at the midpoint when I saw what looked like a fork in the trail. I veered left and got about ten steps onto that path.

Mori Mori and me running on a cold, clear morning in the Atacama Desert.

"Matt, Matt!" I heard behind me, in an unmistakable voice.

I turned and saw Mori Mori running in the same general direction, but he was pointing toward the other path, the one I hadn't taken.

Shit! Wrong way!

I backtracked and ran onto the same trail Mori Mori was on, and as we got shoulder to shoulder, I stuck a hand out onto his arm, smiled, and said, "Thank you," with direct eye contact, more emphasis than usual, so he knew I really appreciated his help. He easily could have let me lose several minutes.

We continued on and he was so close I could hear his footsteps. We hit a rocky stretch, into and among thin channels through two-story-high rock formations. When we emerged, we started a descent, and I heard a loud *CRASH* behind me.

That's bad, I thought.

I stopped, turned to see Mori Mori had taken a rough fall. He wasn't bloodied, but he looked banged up, so I ran back and helped him onto his feet.

"Okay?" I asked him when he was eye level.

"Good now," he said. We nodded and turned back to run.

Mori Mori slowed down after the fall, maybe from the shock. I finished the rest of the stage a few minutes ahead of him, tying with Rob Ripley for second place. Bilbo Baggins outran us all for a strong first-place finish.

Running over some of the nicer terrain in the Atacama Desert.

I was in great spirits. My left shoulder was bruised from my pack, and my right foot was bruised too. But Reinhold came in fifteen minutes behind me. I really saw I could hold my own against the two guys I was measuring myself against—Mori Mori and Reinhold, the ones who beat me by hours and hours and hours in the Namib.

Physically, I could also attest to the fact that the Atacama was really high and really dry. It took me about three and a half hours to finish the course, and I looked like I did not sweat a drop. Sweat evaporated before you knew it, and all that was left was a smear of salt where the sweat would have been.

I walked over to tent #3, nicknamed "Beter," for a nearby archaeological site that had revealed knowledge about the Atacama Desert's earliest inhabitants. They had lived in family-clan groups known as "ayllus," the backbones of their communities.

My little family for the week, my tentmates, included three English-speaking military types. Sean had been a British soldier and now did security contracting work. Mark, a businessman from New Zealand, finished third at the Gobi Race in 2016. And Jack, the ex–Brit soldier who'd just spent the better part of four months rowing the Atlantic.

With Mark from New Zealand (#26) and Jack from Great Britain (tattoo) in front of our tent home in the Atacama Desert.

Sean and Mark and Jack and I talked and talked and talked. And whenever any of those three got up to head out of the tent, they asked if I needed anything (i.e., water). They were great company.

We were all in the tent talking about the day when Jack turned the conversation to one of the toughest races in the running world, the Badwater 135-mile run, which goes through Death Valley in California in July.

"I would never want to run in a place called Death Valley," Jack said.

"Jack, I hate to break it to you," I replied, "but tomorrow's stage is through Valle de la Muerte—the Valley of Death."

"Fuck, mate, I forgot."

We laughed.

The jokes reminded me how cool this race format is. They take place over six stages. At a normal race, you show up, run hard, try to bury the competition, then head home. The other runners on the course are just in the way—less human, more like cones on the course, something to avoid, part of the environment.

In a stage race, naturally on arrival, you meet everyone and wonder how they'll do and if you'll be able to beat this person or that person.

But after the first stage and those thoughts fade away, you quickly recognize who you'll likely run near for the week. You chat with them on the course or after the stage and acknowledge their effort, because it basically mirrors your own. You see them struggling with their pack as much as you are with yours. You learn about their kids, their health problems, their life problems, and they turn from a competitor into something a little different. That's one major ingredient in what makes this race format work.

Another is that the races are hard. They are really hard. You have to travel internationally to get to RacingThePlanet events. You train and prepare for months. You pick out your calories and figure out what you'll eat all week. And then you arrive, and that's when you do that first stage, and then the second, and then you don't want to get up for the third. That's when you realize how hard this all is.

The only people to commiserate with are those who you're supposed to be competing against, and so you say, "Oh well," and instead of treating your fellow competitors like enemies, you realize they're the only ones who really know what you're going through, and so they become your new best friends. It's amazing how quickly a few dozen strangers transform into a few dozen besties, but it does happen and it happens quickly. Under a week, every time.

"Good night," I said to my tentmates, my new best buds, and shut my eyes to thoughts of the Valley of Death.

I tapped the blue square on another cold morning under the yellow banner for a twenty-four-mile second stage. Sam counted us down, this time in English: "3, 2, 1, GO!"

We started the day on flat, straight, dusty roads and about three miles in hit a steep drop into what looked like a river.

Water?

But as we got down we saw the canyon was deep though the water was far shallower compared to the raging river it may have been long, long ago.

The Slot Canyons.

"Slot Canyons" was the stage's nickname, and now we were in them. The race officials had set the course to zigzag through the water, weaving us back and forth, for five full miles. We ran a few hundred yards sometimes, or maybe just a few yards, then crashed back into the ice-cold water up to our waists, crossed to hit dirt on the other shore, then repeated the process.

Hundreds of times. We leapt into and out of the water for miles and miles. The first few crossings I fell hard, and once my shoulder touched river-rock bottom. I popped up, hurt, but also angry, really angry, with myself.

"Step . . . step," I said, out loud, to nobody but myself, as I made the next crossing—a verbal tick to get me to slow myself down, to recognize that I could either rush to failure or recognize that slow was smooth and smooth was fast.

I kept going, back and forth, saying little mental prayers that the cold water crossings would end soon. My hands were so numb that I stuck both down into the sides of my shorts to keep them warm and mobile.

I failed. When I finally emerged from the last water crossing, I came to the checkpoint still shivering. I reached to grab my water bottle from my chest harness, but my fingers wouldn't work the way they should have, and in the handoff to the volunteer at the checkpoint I broke the bottle's straw.

The bottle normally sat upright in my chest harness so the straw would be adjacent to my mouth. Whenever I wanted a sip, I simply pushed the straw over and took a drink.

That system was now busted thanks to my busted bottle. I now had to carry the bottle tucked under my arm like a football for the next fifteen miles. Not exactly ergonomic.

The Slot Canyons made it so we never really could see who was in front of us. I never saw either Bilbo Baggins or Mori Mori, both of whom finished ahead of me. I came in third on the day, but I was still in second overall by about three minutes over Mori Mori.

Bad news of the night: Sean was hurt, something in his chest didn't feel right. He told us he thought he'd be out. Our tent might be one man down already.

Confirmed. Sean was out, but we all had to kick on so we were back under the yellow banner, I was tapping my blue. Sam was counting down.

I felt like I wanted out too. The day had some truly terrible terrain. It came in several varieties. "Trap door" dirt looked solid but you would fall in as deep as your knee. Terra cotta–like clay flipped up in dinner-plate-sized sheets and hit your shins. Fields of "frozen broccoli"—petrified short grass shaped into points. Patches of calcified coral remnants that were also super sharp. Rock piles, lava rock, shrubs stiff as a schoolmarm's switch. I got down on all fours to crawl straight up two sand dunes.

Today's twenty-four-mile stage was nicknamed for the ancient Atacameños Trail, the one the far-back ancestors took to traverse the great desert. We also passed ALMA—the Atacama Large Millimeter/submillimeter Array—at 16,000 feet, with sixty-six radio telescopes, fully operational since 2013 in an international partnership with several space-gazing countries. So today contained some old and some new.

Running past a mountain in the Atacama Desert.

I staggered to the finish. Mori Mori put nine minutes on me, and now he had overtaken me for second place overall. I was covered in salt and gulped down a liter of water in sixty seconds at the finish line. I felt like shit.

I sat on a foldout stool at the finish, not moving except to suck water. I glanced over to camp and saw Mori Mori bouncing with the pep of a teenager on a first lawn-mowing job.

It's over, I thought. *He's back.*

I dragged myself to my tent and lay there for hours. I just wanted out of the sun because it was so powerful. After a while, Jack came in, Mark not far behind. At 2 PM the wind picked up and the tents flapped back and forth, louder and louder, until 3 PM, when our tent looked like it might fly away. We secured our stuff, putting everything back in our bags.

"You think this can get any worse?" Jack asked, grinning the grin of a guy who knew that yes, absolutely, it could get worse.

Then it did.

We heard shouting outside. And then: "Evacuate! Evacuate!" That's a word that gets your ears up. I put on my sunglasses and pulled my neck gaiter over my mouth, poked my head outside. I could not see a thing.

The sand moved so fast the sky was gone. Swirling tan. It was early afternoon and we were in a weird beige twilight. A race official came to our tent.

"Get your stuff, get to a truck!" she shouted and pointed toward the white quad cabs the race used to move camp every day.

"Where are we going?" I shouted back over the noise.

"Don't know! Not here!"

Our tent was caving at this point, where we used to stand we could only duck to half height. If we stayed longer we'd be crawling.

I grabbed my running shoes in hand and, wearing sandals, threw on my pack, making my way to the truck while bits of sand hit me everywhere like tiny, hot hail. I had trouble seeing through it all but spotted a truck with a door that had just slammed shut. Since it hadn't driven off yet I figured it must still have a spot left.

What is that? That sound? I thought while I made my way to the truck. *It's the drums!* The race drums were still beating—in a sandstorm!

I grabbed the truck-door handle, opened it, and found Anim from South Africa and Jodi from Alaska inside. The driver was Chilean, didn't speak English, so he couldn't tell us where we were going. We drove through the sandstorm for twenty minutes until we emerged somewhere less windy and sandy, then continued twenty minutes more to an old adobe schoolhouse.

It took time for the trucks to shuttle the runners back and forth to our school safe house, so it wasn't until nightfall when we learned what was going on. One of the trucks brought Reinhold in, limping on a crutch, with a badly swollen leg. During the sandstorm he'd been hit with an enormous flying wooden table, had to be rushed to a hospital, where they told him he would be out the rest of the week. When I saw him I gave him a hug and my genuine condolences. Another competitor couldn't see through the sand, fell hard, and required five stitches to close up his forehead.

When I took stock I was physically okay but mentally drained. My energy was low, dangerously low—so low that though I was starving and needed to get hot water to make my dehydrated meal, I couldn't even do that and gave up and just ate an entire 800-calorie bag of chili-flavored Wonderful pistachios, crawled into my small sack on the schoolhouse's concrete floor, closed my eyes, and wished I was somewhere, anywhere, other than there.

I woke to Jodi and John.

Jodi was a force of nature. She was up, smiling, talking to everyone, smiling some more, chatting about climbing mountains (while smiling) and the triathlon she planned to do down in Patagonia after this race. There was an energy to her I could feel five feet away, and it was a little contagious.

"We're not racing today. They need a day to reset the course, so we'll do Stage 4 tomorrow," Jodi told me.

"Did you really just eat pistachios last night? You okay?" asked John.

"Yes to the first. Not sure about the second." *The former was the truth, the latter was a little lie. Something was wrong. I didn't want to say it though.*

Maybe John knew. He seemed to chat me up more than usual, paying closer attention, checking in, and when he saw I couldn't stop sniffing his homemade couscous and eggs, he asked, "Want some?"

"John, I would seriously give you my other kidney for that right now."

I sat down with that bag of couscous and eggs, and the world melted away. I shoveled bite after bite after bite for the few minutes it took until the bag was empty and my stomach was full.

I wandered to where the race kept the "Cyber Café." Typically it was in a tent, but there they had set out two computers in what looked to be the school's cafeteria. I'd been so busy running and thinking about Mori Mori that I'd only had time to fire out a couple updates via email. I hadn't seen a single inbound message yet. I clicked a couple times and had to sit to brace myself.

I found seventy messages waiting for me. Family, friends, college classmates and old acquaintances, work colleagues and grade school pals—all answered my pre-race plea for help. One woman wrote, "the whole world is watching and supporting you," and for a moment, in that adobe school in the Atacama Desert, it felt that way. People told me they were praying for me, including the minister who had baptized my daughters. Big Theo wrote from the Netherlands. My mom wrote. Heck, my mother-in-law wrote.

My old commander from Iraq wrote, "You're an inspiration . . . Keep running man."

A volunteer from the Namib wrote, "What you're doing is so incredibly inspiring, and such a role model for anyone who's questioning what they can achieve, or whether they should go after the crazy goals . . . All of us who have met you are cheerleading you around the globe, sending you all best thoughts and wishes."

Rachel wrote, several times, and seemed worried: "Have a good—not sure 'good' is the right word—day tomorrow . . . sleep well and keep moving forward. Love you, Rachel."

There were so many others that needed to check messages too, so I didn't have time to read them all. I scanned just enough to make a mental list for who I should be ready to respond to. I wrote a list of names, and as

I moved down the messages, I saw a long one from someone I was certain I didn't know. Curious, I clicked on the message.

Matt,

You are an inspiration.

I hope this message gives you some strength, because you have done that time and again for me without even knowing me. I'm scheduled for a non-directed kidney donation surgery next Wednesday 10/5. Very soon after I made the decision to see if I qualified for donating, I discovered your blog posts and your story. I've been a casual runner all my life and finally kicked it up a notch and finished my first marathon this year. You've been the person I think about every time I have doubt about the surgery and its impact on me or my goals to keep running marathons or bump up to trail races or ultras. Keep crushing it, and I hope that fate throws us together at the starting line of a race one day.

Best,
Bryce

I read it. I read it again. I reread it. I smiled—thought, *people can see this*—looked around the dusty school building and felt like I had wings, like walking wasn't walking anymore. I could fly.

I felt full. The meal and the messages changed everything.

It was a windy morning but not sandstorm windy. We were to run the infamous salt flats today, out into the great, wide-open Atacama Desert for about twenty-three miles.

I felt good, so good I almost forgot to tap my blue square under the yellow banner, and Sam did her countdown, and we were off.

Stage 4 in the Atacama, the morning after Jodi's positivity, John's generosity, and all those kind messages that filled me back up.

I fell in near Mori Mori for a while, but then I took off and he couldn't catch me. Jack looked like he'd been jump-started with a car battery and ran with me through the midpoint, Mori Mori behind us. Both of us being from military backgrounds, Jack cracked me up when he alerted me Mori wasn't far back.

"Zero on your tail, mate," he said, a reference to the feared World War II Japanese fighter planes. His perfect timing doubled me over with laughter.

We kept on and I dropped Jack to move into second. We ran around this huge water hole, and toward the end of the stage we looped back onto the same stretch of road we had just run, where I passed Mori Mori going the other way. We made eye contact. I held my face stern, shedding strain, so he would see I wasn't done yet.

The water hole in the Atacama Desert, near the finish of Stage 4.

Down a bit further, I saw my tentmate Mark, the New Zealander. I passed him and said, "Ka Mate," a phrase I knew he'd know as part of the famous Māori haka, sung at All Blacks rugby matches, an expression meaning "until death." He smiled.

I pressed the pace as hard as I could, to a speed I hadn't held so late in the week at the end of a stage, but I wanted to put time on him.

At the finish line I smiled and waited for Mori Mori. The longer he took, the closer I got to maybe even overtaking him. He came in three minutes after me, so I had knocked his lead down to only a couple minutes overall, as close as we could get.

My legs were cut up, my back had opened up again, and I was so covered in salt that the American flag patch on my shoulder looked like the red stripes had disappeared in all the extra white.

But I still had some spring in my step. And I would need it.

The Long March toward La Valle de la Luna (Valley of the Moon) was expected to be forty-six miles, my third long stage this year. Sam, aside the yellow banner, reminded us to be careful, I rubbed my blue square extra hard, we got another "tres, dos, uno . . . GO," and we ran off.

I just wanted to stay ahead of Mori Mori. All I could think about was keeping that yellow hat and orange shirt behind me. He still had that balled-up giant cheek thing going on, and I made a mental note to ask him about it.

The day went according to plan, until we came to the midpoint. There was a checkpoint at the top of a rise, above a small canyon. When I crested the hill, the volunteers revealed a prize: the Coke! It was unexpected; I swilled it in seconds. I ran down the hill and turned left into the canyon.

I followed the canyon half a mile, maybe more, and couldn't spot a pink pin flag.

Something's not right, I thought.

I decided to keep running straight, but I scanned more as I approached the canyon's end. I could now see back to the checkpoint, off in the distance, and if I squinted, I saw a flash of yellow and orange.

What? Wait, what? Mori Mori!

Instantly I realized, *I'm off course!*

I sprinted back into the small canyon to the turnoff from the checkpoint, looked left, and saw a small crack in the canyon where there was a single pink pin flag where I should have turned.

That's where Mori went, I thought, and realized I had to follow.

Now he's ahead.

That was all it took. One mistake, and he pounced. I never saw Mori Mori again, and he cruised ahead over that second half and put a huge margin on me.

I finished third overall.

It was a washing-machine week—emotions all over, down and up and sideways. And so when I saw the finish line, the drums beating, and Amelia was there—my newfound distant South African aunt who'd first checked my bag in the Namib and had been at all the races this year—I hugged her a little too tight, as if her arms included all those others that sent support from so far away, as if her fingers were Georgie's, were Grace's, were Rachel's. I needed that hug. Because I was spent, because I'd lost something, because I'd won something, because, for once, for now, I felt like people out there noticed that I was running past the end of me and that it was starting to make an actual difference. My running was helping to save lives.

It was finally working.

The next morning everyone was happy. We went through the normal routine—our yellow banner, Sam counted us down, I tapped my girls' baby blanket—but we all knew it was just a five-mile jog to the final finish. I ran with a pack of eight guys including my tentmates Jack and Mark, jaw-jacking the whole way, and we came in across the finish line together, arms up; I held Rob Ripley's hand to the sky as we crossed.

I was elated. Someone from the race staff told us that Bilbo Baggins (Rob) had set the Atacama Crossing record by a clear margin, which meant this year was an outlier. There had been sixteen Atacama Crossings to date, and I learned I would have won the race every year except this record-setting year and 2012 (so fourteen out of sixteen Atacama Crossings, of course, setting aside Mori Mori's performance this week). I would have beaten the South African ultrarunning champ Ryan Sandes in 2010 by minutes, and the great Dean Karnazes in 2008 by hours. That's partly unfair to Ryan and Dean—I'd be the first to acknowledge year-to-year comparisons are inherently off because the course and weather conditions are so variable. But I used their times merely as a marker to measure against—and to know that with one kidney, I could still compete at a high level in rough conditions.

John and me at the final finish line in the Atacama Desert. (Having run the race mostly on one leg, he earned that smile.)

We bused back to San Pedro de Atacama, cleaned up, and there wasn't much time to walk the few blocks to the restaurant where we would have our banquet. I found the "La Casona" sign ("Big House") and walked into a beautiful, big open courtyard with elegantly appointed wooden picnic tables. Dinner was heavy on the meat, and everyone toasted with a pisco sour (or three), a local favorite drink, to celebrate. After dinner was mostly over, Sam took the microphone and announced winners in different categories.

When she got to the open men competition, Sam said, "In third place, running with one kidney, is Matt Cavanaugh from the United States." John was next to me chanting "USA, USA!" I walked up to Mary, also onstage, and she handed me a silver plate. I leaned in to hug her. And then I just started to talk. I'd thought hard about what to say, but I didn't have any notes, so it was from the heart:

> Everything you need to know about the volunteers, the medical staff, the paid staff, and the local staff, from this past week, is that when the

sandstorm came, the drum kept beating. From the depths of my heart, genuinely, we can't do what we love to do unless you do what you do. You endure just as much as we do, so thank you, very much, from all the runners.

You know, before this race, I looked at some very old maps of this desert and they say "there be dragons." And that's perfect for a RacingThePlanet event. Because we come here to slay dragons. I've done two of these this year, and when I go home, nobody's ever asked me what my time was. I doubt anyone asks you what your time is, because when you come here, you come here to do something much bigger. You don't come here and just get a time, you come home with stories, and those stories matter.

And another thing about slaying dragons, with apologies to myths and movies, is that you don't do it alone. You never do.

So in Namibia—Reinhold, I was suffering, and you opened your bag up and you showed me how you do this. You looked at my bag, and you said, "Matt, why do you have a bag for another bag?" Mori Mori, on the first day—you barely speak English, but you yelled my name when I was ahead of you, to keep me on the course. You easily could have let me lose ten seconds (or more). A minute later, when you fell, I stopped because it sounded bad and I helped you back up. I'd like to think I pushed you a little this week.

Jack, Mark, Sean, you are perfect company when you're stuck in the middle of fucking nowhere. You guys are amazing. Fastest tent in this crowd (after Sean got sick).

And John, John Bezou is right here in front of me, over the course of this year has become a very good friend, and I would never be standing here if it wasn't for him.

Beyond that, holding this award right here, when I start deducting the percentages that I owe to all of you, for your encouragement and your inspiration, I only have a minority stake in this thing. So thank you to all of you for pushing me this week.

> I've got one last tiny thought. One year ago, almost exactly one year ago, I donated my left kidney. I was able to save a stranger in Seattle's life, and then help an additional seven people along the way. But I'm not the only one that does this. Jodi in the back, you've all met her. [A pause for riotous applause.] There's an organization called Kidney Donor Athletes, there's a thousand members that have done the same thing. And if I can leave you with one thought, it's this—for an awful lot of people out there, that are out there right now, that are getting closer and closer to death—you are the cure. All of you. If you can make it through this week, you can donate a kidney, and I'm standing right here as living proof, you can continue to do these things just as well as you did before. So if you choose that route, to follow those pink flags, I promise you it'll lead somewhere that'll make your life a whole helluva lot better.
>
> Thank you so much, it was an honor to run with you this week.

The rest of the night went by too fast, but I saw Gemma, the British nurse living in Ohio, at the bar.

"How was your week?" I asked. It was only then I realized I hadn't seen her all week.

"I got Covid." She frowned.

"You what?"

"Yeah," she went on. "I came up positive before the week even started. I was stuck in the hotel for five days and only got out a day ago. So I'm going to have to come back."

I couldn't believe it. Such a near miss. Chances were, when we spent hours next to one another chatting away, she had Covid all the while, and I was super exposed. But somehow, because we had taken precautions, I hadn't caught it, tested negative, raced, and had a week beyond belief.

It's not just the banquet speech that got me thinking about how many others helped me this week. It was something a first sergeant I served with used to say: "We ain't got heroes around here, we got teammates." He meant we can't do anything important or big by ourselves.

After an avalanche of support like that, an infusion of hope, I finished third overall. Bronze felt like gold to me considering the field of fast, talented runners in that race.

I crossed the Atacama Desert without someone beside me. But I was never alone.

And dragons don't ever really go extinct, because when you've slayed one, you go on to find the next. In six weeks I would leave to find the last one this year—in Antarctica. In the snow. The Last Desert, the White Desert, the fourth and final event in the Grand Slam.

ACTION THIS DAY

"There be dragons" was always metaphorical. There are no actual dragons. Even if everyone didn't know it then (or now). But dragons exist. They can't be seen, only felt. They don't have wings or tails, fire or teeth. They are the problems that seem too big. The fear we don't want to face. The pain that looks unbearable. The challenge that appears too great.

The goal, then, is simple. It's not about times or scores, it's about getting the job done, slaying the dragon, no matter how ugly it might look or feel. The most important lesson is to know that you cannot slay a dragon alone.

Everyone plays a part. Even those not directly engaged in the combat, even those who start but don't make it all the way to the end help the others that do.

Leadville Trail 100 Run founder Ken Chlouber famously suggested, "Make friends with pain and you'll never be alone." Others talk about going into a personal "pain cave" at endurance events. Some take it as a sort of solitary confinement, as in, *just you and the hurtin' and get used to it.*

But there's a second meaning many miss. Move the emphasis just a little—"Make friends" [pause] "with pain"—and this instead reminds us to spend time with others in pain and that puts our own in perspective. We often get so locked on our own pain that we forget others are in rough spots too. That shift helps us see our own troubles aren't so troubling, our own hurts don't hurt so bad. We suffer better together. We can break out of the pain cave and instead make it a pain party. That's another way we benefit from our fellow dragon slayers.

So—what's your dragon, and who's going to help you cut it down?

Chapter Nine

CHOOSE THE HARDER RIGHT OVER THE EASIER WRONG

Rarely is the easy choice the right choice.

October 3, 2022
George Bush Intercontinental/Houston Airport

Time is running out.

That flashed through my head at the Houston airport.

What inevitably happens at these races is that all the runners depart from the same minuscule airport in places without any street signs, dozens of us clumped together in a tiny terminal with exactly one vending machine. The group progressively flies on to a larger airport, a hub like a Munich or a Santiago, where a few trickle off here, a few trickle off there, a sort of sorting happens based on destination. The group gets smaller and smaller, down to five, down to four, down to three, and then it's just you and the last new friend you made the previous week. These races don't end so much as they fade away.

It happened to me again, this time in Houston, third time this year. This time I said my final goodbye to Trish of Canada, a short-haired spark of kindness who had a tough week (she was in the top few women but had to pull out due to sickness) yet was nonetheless cheerful. I wished her all the best, hugged her off, then turned to my own flight.

And suddenly, after all that, after the Atacama Desert, I was all alone.

I walked to my gate, boarded, and, knowing I needed to stay awake to get my body back on schedule, I put on a movie.

It was called *Explorer*, a documentary about Sir Ranulph Fiennes, the British adventurer who had set several polar exploration records and Guinness World Records and lived an extraordinary life. Fiennes was a military officer and went on to tackle great adventures and write books. As I watched, it felt like the universe was shooting up a star for me to follow.

For instance, it wasn't hard to notice that others, many others, thought Fiennes's decision to take risks and set records was foolish. On a three-year odyssey around the globe, one critic in the film said Fiennes was "out there for the wrong reasons." Another: "How insecure do you need to be to go around the fucking world to beat the rival to feel good about yourself?"

My sympathies were with Fiennes. Here was someone who became a role model to me in the span of a flight. Someone to look up to. Fiennes even suggested what felt like direct personal advice:

> I got brought up with a religion but not strong enough to deal with gangrene and crotch rot and all that sort of stuff. So I have to invent my own way of having a mental fight. And that is to say people I respected most in my life, my father and my grandfather, are watching me and I must not give in. I must not give in. I invite the ghosts into my head so they are there and I do not want to let them down.

Mental note for mental fights: *Invite the ghosts.*

Don't let them down.

Forty-seven days to departure for Antarctica.

I hung up the phone and smiled.

She called me. We spoke for two hours about everything and nothing. I was still in Colorado; she was in Utah with the girls. After a long day of work and school, kids tucked in, she'd rung me out of the blue. It was one of those calls where you're talking so long you have to make your way over to bed because you know it's the last thing you'll do before you fall asleep, and the conversation only ends when the sleep begins.

Rachel—or at least, Rachel's voice—sounded like it had at the beginning. Like us again. And that was all I ever wanted, really, her attention, to feel it shine on me. For so long I'd felt like I was on the dark side of her moon, less worthy of affection than the dog.

But this felt good. Things were good. Being in Utah, nearer her family, she seemed at ease. I thought maybe since the environment changed, perhaps things had also changed for us. She'd even left me a "totem" in the bathroom while I was visiting Utah—an inside joke, a little "man" made up of my shaving cream bottle, Tylenol jar, toothbrush, night-light, comb, and other bathroom items.

Twenty-four days to departure for Antarctica.

Despite the approaching race in Antarctica, I had to go to the Florida Keys for a kidney-donation nonprofit event. On the flight down I thought about the challenge to come.

As excited as I was about the Atacama Crossing, I was now even further behind Ben Dame for the 4 Deserts Champion trophy. Mori Mori and I were now tied—my fourth (Namib), third (Georgia), and third (Atacama) = 4 + 3 + 3 = 10. Mori Mori's second, sixth, and second = 2 + 6 + 2 = 10. While I had hoped to put Mori Mori down in the Atacama, we instead emerged equal. Ben's magic number stood at 7, so no matter what, he had an enormous lead on both of us for the trophy.

Of course this format was unfair to us Grand Slammers, but them's the breaks.

In order to win, I would need to win Antarctica, which would put me ahead of Mori Mori. Then simultaneously I had to hope Ben finished fourth or worse because that would put me up on him too. (My magic number in that scenario would be 11, his would be 11 or worse, and I would win because I'd have finished ahead of Ben at Antarctica.) Both were tall orders, especially since Mori Mori had beaten me twice over the year, and the only time I got him was when he was sick as a chocolate-eating dog.

Maybe winning was impossible, and I was just too stupid and stubborn to see it.

Then there was word going around on Antarctica that you could treat it like a fun run. A big victory lap, celebrating the series finish with a sightseeing jog.

Instead of austere camps and pit toilets, we would be aboard a relatively luxurious ship with beds for sleeping, a dining hall for eating, and even a bar for drinking (though against race rules, I'm sure some runners would sneak the booze anyway). I had pledged to be the first kidney donor to Grand Slam the series—I was shocked I had made it this far—so merely getting to the final finish would fulfill my promise. I never promised I'd win. And besides, my body was already beaten, bloodied, fatigued.

Not only that, racing Antarctica would be different from all the events so far. Off the sand, onto the snow, away from the scorpions, on to the penguins. I would have to deal with crossing the Drake Passage, inbound and outbound, notoriously the roughest seas on the planet.[36] (I have gotten sick on a flat-water ferry before.)

---

36 After the race we learned another ship like ours had a passenger fatality from a "rogue wave" in the Drake, and that ship had to return to port for an investigation of the death.

I'd never run on snow and ice for so long, and I would have to wear Microspikes the entire time. We were told the weather could roll in at any time and stop a stage (or two or maybe more). I didn't know how it would go.

This would be an entirely new race. Nothing I had learned would apply. I'd have to completely change my gear and approach.

So why not take it easy? Don't push too hard. Just finish.

On arrival in the Florida Keys, on the sidelines of the presentations and talks, this was all I thought about. And everyone there, in the relatively small living kidney-donor world, seemed to want to talk about Antarctica too. I had several conversations with kind and well-meaning folks who, nonetheless, reinforced the thought that I should take Antarctica easy.

One told me point-blank he thought it wasn't "normal" to run so hard so soon after donation, and he encouraged me to consider dropping out of the last event because I had already "proven" my point. Another told me to back off, that a race like this wasn't "worth getting hurt." And then: "Who's going to know if you just jog it in? Nobody will know except some penguins."

The entire time on this trip to Florida, the reasons against running hard in Antarctica kept piling like logs on a bonfire.

I thought, *You're too far back to catch Ben.*

Even if you do, Mori Mori will win anyway.

You got good at running the deserts; this is different.

You're gonna be too seasick to run.

You'll get hurt.

Just finish; that's enough.

It's Antarctica, so far away that nobody will know.

Just have fun.

It was hard to argue. I thought harder about taking this last one easy.

Seven days to departure for Antarctica.

A phone call can change everything.

Mary Gadams, RacingThePlanet's CEO, had invited Dean Karnazes (the author of *Ultramarathon Man* and the hero of mine who got me into running) to attempt to be the first to Grand Slam the 4 Deserts series in 2008 (he would also win the 4 Deserts Champion trophy that year). He blazed a trail there just as he has so many other times. He's become famous for flipping the popular acronym FKT ("fastest known time") into "first known time."

I got lucky in that Mary put Dean and me in contact because I needed some last-minute tips from the best of the best. So I called.

We talked for an hour. It was mostly chitchat, the usual small talk runners engage in. But it had a grown-up fanboy dimension as well. I wanted to tell him how he'd impacted my life, my health, my everything, but I fumbled. I think he still sensed it regardless.

Dean told me about a problem he'd had with scopolamine, the coin-sized patches like little Band-Aids people put behind their ears to counter the effects of seasickness. He asked if I was going to use them, and, not knowing of their existence until that very moment, I fibbed and said, "Of course." Dean counseled me to take it off a day before the first race. He'd made the mistake of leaving his on after crossing the Drake Passage, and it seriously impacted his vision, which in turn impacted his ability to run. His first stage was shot because he'd left a tiny patch on the skin behind his ear.

"Thank you, man, really," I said. "I'll be sure to get mine off. It's amazing what havoc such a small thing can cause."

He agreed, then pivoted to ask loads of his own questions about kidney donation with deep sincerity and curiosity. I told him my story.

"I think you're brave," he said.

If ever there was a moment when the mic dropped and time stopped, it was hearing a hero of mine express that he'd heard enough of my life to consider me "brave." Like Superman calling you "super."

Imagine you're me for a second. You had a rough day. Something didn't work out. Then the world sends you a sign. It reminds you somehow that—once—you did something brave. Once you suspended your own self-interest for someone's greater good. Once you saved a life.

You can't stay mad or down for too long when the world won't let you. That's a superpower waiting on the other side of kidney donation. It took a call with Dean to show me that.

The Cadet Prayer at West Point advises cadets to "choose the harder right over the easier wrong." It's a simple saying about the difficult trade-offs in life. We all encounter these moments. Rarely is the easy choice the right choice.

My dad showed me that. Like all the cool kids in middle school, I had braces, which meant I had to go in periodically for adjustments. This life milestone coincided with the age I achieved my driver's permit, so one day, Dad let me drive home from the orthodontist. It was a pretty safe and uncomplicated driving trip home for the rookie behind the wheel.

What Dad didn't know was that I had twisted my right ankle playing soccer. I tried to press the accelerator pedal with my left foot, and as I backed out, my inexperienced off-foot pressure was too hard, I jammed the pedal down too far, which caused me to freak out and turn the car's front end too far to the right, which slammed our front end straight into a brand-new sports car. I put the car in park, still in contact with the sports car after impact.

I looked at Dad. Dad looked at me. The parking lot was full of cars but completely devoid of people. It would have been so easy for Dad to hop into the driver's seat and drive off, leaving the damage anonymous to the sports car's owner. It would have been even easier since the office complex was massive, meaning he'd have to visit multiple floors and open multiple doors to find the damaged car's owner. He would have to work hard to actually find someone inside to pay money to for a mistake he himself didn't make.

But that was what he did. It seemed like he was in that building forever before he successfully located the car's owner,[37] exchanged insurance information, and came back out to deliver his shamed son back to school. He must have thought this was so unfair; he easily could have cursed me out, but he didn't. He got on with it. Dad chose the harder right over the easier wrong.

It made no sense to anybody else, but it might have made sense to Ranulph, Dean, my dad, or even H. L. Mencken, who once wrote, "Every normal man must be tempted, at times, to spit on his hands, hoist the black flag, and begin slitting throats."

Exactly. I had a million bad reasons to go easy, a few powerful ones to go hard, but in the end it was just me and me alone who could make the decision to pull the trigger.

Screw the lazy wrong. I'm going to win this whole fucking thing.

Two days to departure for Antarctica.

ACTION THIS DAY

All of us live right on that razor's edge between the tougher right and effortless wrong.

The difference between the two is often purpose. What're you doing it for? Why?

To be pulled by purpose is the greatest gift you can give yourself. To know why you're doing something. To know the reason. To feel it deeply. There is no more motivating spark than that.

---

37 Dad later told me that when he went into the office complex, he went room to room asking, "Does anyone own a new red sports car?" He found the owner when someone finally responded, "Do I *want* to own a red sports car?"

When you donate a kidney, you're always reminded about it. Your family knows—you can hardly hide a hospital stay without symptoms of illness. Your co-workers know—you can't skip work without word slipping out. And every time you get into the shower or visit the sea you'll look down and see the scars. Even if you tried, you could not forget having donated.

It provides an inescapable sense of purpose, a reminder all at once at how precious life is and, at your best, how powerful you can be in preventing pain to others. In this case, it helped guide me to race for the win, even though that would be the far harder path.

How can you embrace your harder right?

Chapter Ten

THROUGH ENDURANCE WE CONQUER

RACE ACROSS THE LAST DESERT—ANTARCTICA

Through endurance we conquer (fortitudine vincimus).

—Sir Ernest Shackleton

November 20, 2022
Ministro Pistarini International Airport
Buenos Aires, Argentina

"Julita!"

I saw Julita near the gate we'd arrived into—she'd dyed electric-blue streaks into her already-emphatic long, yellow blonde hair. Paired with her giant smile, she was practically glowing, even after a long flight from Poland. John and Karen Bezou showed up soon after. Karen had come to see John race at the bottom of the earth. And Doreen arrived too, who had run in the Namib (and witnessed John peel a skin sheet off my back).

We flew from Buenos Aires south to Tierra del Fuego ("land of fire"), an archipelago which includes Ushuaia, a city that never let you forget where you were. Everywhere you went signs proclaimed "fin del mundo" ("end of the world"), which didn't feel like an exaggeration. The city looked like South America's Valhalla, a steroidal Alaska, with blue water surrounded by sharp mountain peaks.

After a short stay in Ushuaia, on the afternoon of November 22, we boarded the *Hondius*. As a ship made to break ice, it had a blocky, industrial look, but inside it felt like a hotel.

I'd never been on a cruise ship, so I explored to get my bearings. We would be on this thing for close to two weeks.[38] There were nearly 250 people on board—75 crew and staff, 115 tourists, and then 55 affiliated with the race in some way.[39] The ship operated as a floating base camp. For the tourists on board, each day there were several activities to sign up for over the course of the week on the Antarctic Peninsula, including kayaking, mountaineering, snowshoeing, photography, rubber boat cruising (using inflatable ten-person military-grade motorboats known as "Zodiacs"), and overnight camping on the snow.

I was on Deck 4, the same level as the main entry to the ship and the dining room. Below us was Deck 3, where a lot of race-affiliated cabins were, and where we found the doors that would take us out to the Zodiacs. On Deck 5 there was a big open lounge with observation windows and a bar (though we were reminded repeatedly we were not allowed to drink until the race was over). Deck 5 also had a meeting room where we gathered for information about the next day's stage.

---

38 It would take 2.5 days at sea to arrive at the Antarctic Peninsula. We anticipated being in and around the peninsula for seven days. Then approximately 2.5 days in transit back to Ushuaia. We were told these timelines were all weather dependent.

39 The crew took care of the ship's functions; the staff were more like adventure tour guides.

My roommate was a perfect match. We seemed to want to chat at the same time, rest at the same time, wander the ship at the same time. It was great. His name was Ed. He was around sixty, had worked a full career in Singapore in financial services, and, though originally from the Northeast US, had now had settled in Denver. He was a cold-weather ultramarathon junkie, with plans to run 120 miles above the Arctic Circle in coming months. John and Karen were down the hall from Ed and me.

Our room on Deck 4 was small but superb. Loads of storage in wall cabinets. It had the feel of a functional tiny house at sea. We had our own bathroom and a sizable porthole that foregrounded the outdoor walkway and kept the cold ocean in the background.

The *Hondius* passed through the Beagle Channel, so named for the British ship that would later become world-famous through its even more famous passenger, Charles Darwin.

The shaking began when we hit the Drake Passage, at the intersection of a narrow passage and the world's strongest current. It felt like we were a mouse atop a fire-hose jet stream. A bumpy ride.

As expected, I was seasick. I wasn't as bad as others who were puking everywhere—including Julita, unfortunately—but I did have to stick a scopolamine patch behind my ear. It helped immensely, but it also made me sleepy, dilated my pupils so much it was hard to read and write, and made my throat so dry I had to take cough drops like candy.

"Attention RacingThePlanet runners," blared the intercom. "Meeting on Deck Five in thirty minutes."

I headed up to the meeting room early to check messages. While many things were different about this event, one thing was the same. We were again so remote at the bottom of the planet that internet access was limited, so we used the race email system.

I punched in a few codes and navigated to the inbound messages. The first one I saw was from a stranger:

Dear Mr. Cavanaugh,

I have been following your racing adventure for quite a while now and your story has been very helpful for me. I am a 19-year old college student who really loves outdoor activities like trail running, rock climbing, caving, backpacking, etc. When I was trying to decide whether or not I would be a non-directed donor one of my biggest worries was about my ability to continue on adventures. After graduation I might want to be a medical officer in the military as well as keep up an active lifestyle so your proving how possible it is to push oneself on one kidney pushed me over the edge to decide to call the [National Kidney Registry]. I just got my approval as a donor recently . . .

You said in one of your posts long ago that all of this suffering would be worth it if it convinces just one person that they can be a kidney donor too. I don't know how many other people you have impacted as well but you convinced me that it only takes one. I'm going through with the donation in large part because of you and I want you to know what an impact you have made. Good luck with your race, we folks on the home front will cheer you on and be proud of you whatever happens.

All my best,
Joey

I was speechless. I sat alone, tearing up, stunned. In just the past few weeks I had also received a message from a woman going forward with donation in Calgary, a guy in London doing the same, and now this.

They see this—they see what I'm doing.

I wiped my eyes and wondered, *Will more people donate if I win?*

Runners filtered into the meeting room, screen at front, rows of fixed, couch-like seats facing the screen, until it was standing room only. Mary strode to the front, welcomed us, and she went through the basics.

"This is a race for distance, first and foremost," she told us. "All our other events you run a standard distance and cover it as *fast* as you can for time. Antarctica is different. For safety reasons, you will instead run for a set amount of time and you will try to run as *far* as you can for distance. Each day whoever runs farthest wins the stage."

She explained safety was paramount on Antarctica. The weather rolls in fast, and they had to be able to evacuate the runners quickly. So we would run laps around set loops for distance until the first runner got to 250 kilometers. Weather conditions were our great challenge. In five of the nine years the race had been held, Mary explained, no runner made it to 250 kilometers (155 miles), mostly due to weather. In 2008, the winner recorded only 77 kilometers total, and South African Ryan Sandes won the 2010 event with 230 kilometers.

"There's just one problem," Mary said, breaking some bad news. King George Island in the South Shetlands, just north of the Antarctic Peninsula, was typically where the race aimed for the first stage. That's because King George was home to a number of international science bases, and it had roads that enabled larger, longer, faster loops (up to ten or fifteen kilometers). The safety concerns were lower there, so the race used that stage to jack up the mileage so runners had a boost toward the 250-kilometer goal.

"The captain has told me we will not stop at King George Island. The weather is too bad. So we're headed for Portal Point on the Antarctic Peninsula instead."

Everyone groaned. Things just got a lot harder because the loops just got a lot smaller and slower.

Mary explained some rules. Environmental regulations on Antarctica do not permit solid food or wrappers of any kind, no matter what, period. Having these items, she said, would bring an instant race penalty and maybe disqualification. We were, however, permitted to put calorie-dense drink mix into our hydration bottles in order to take in some liquid calories while running.

A hand went up. "Can we have a cough drop or anything to suck on?" I glanced over at Mori Mori and noticed he had that bulge in his cheek again, like in the Atacama.

"No." Mary's face turned firm. "Absolutely nothing solid. We're lucky to be allowed to hold this race at all and we cannot jeopardize it with any litter whatsoever."

Mori Mori's face went blank. He knew he wouldn't be able to use whatever that substance was, and he wasn't happy about it.

She went on to explain the start/finish setup. We would take the Zodiacs in, land, and walk inland. Somewhere down by the landing site, near the water, the race would set up one or two camp toilets. The race would establish a start/finish area, up and inland from the toilets, where we would change into running shoes, put on our Microspikes and snow gaiters, and then place all our drop bags (with emergency clothing and gear) onto tarps.

At the start/finish, there would be staff and volunteers with hole punchers. Each runner would have a laminated card, and each lap earned one punch. Since each runner was on course for roughly the same amount of time, every runner's objective was to run for as many laps (and distance) as possible in that given amount of time.[40]

"Be prepared for anything," Mary told us at least a half dozen times during the briefing.

We left the meeting thinking we'd depart the ship at 4 AM the next day on the Zodiacs for an early race start (at this time of year on Antarctica, there were over eighteen hours of daylight, so an early start like that would seem, but was not, crazy). We wouldn't know what the course would look like until we hit the snow.

Our first "be prepared for anything" moment came quickly. Late at night we got word we wouldn't depart until 5:30 AM.

---

40 Of course, if they call "stop" and you're still out on a lap, you get to finish that currently in-progress lap and it would count toward your total.

November 25, 2022
Portal Point

Early in the morning, the *Hondius* made it to Portal Point at the front edge of Charlotte Bay, on the Antarctic Peninsula, the "tail" of land that sticks out toward Argentina.

I saw it.

Antarctica. The White Desert. The Last Desert. The size of the United States plus Mexico. Coldest, windiest, highest continent on Earth. Highest because the ice pack is more than a mile deep on average. Ninety percent of Earth's ice. Nearly 80 percent of the world's fresh water. Low precipitation makes Antarctica an actual desert, the world's largest by far. Rigid rules also make this place, in essence, the world's largest nature preserve. The fourth continent I'd raced on this year.

Antarctica's most striking feature was the contrast between white snow and blue water. It is replicated millions of times over in the waters offshore, in the big white jagged blocks that cleaved from the glaciers. Only the largest blocks, greater than five meters, are called "icebergs." The middle-sized ones are "bergy bits" (seriously), the smallest are "growlers."

We got the order to hold—to wait until 6 AM. Then we were waved off completely because the winds were too strong, over forty miles per hour, which might flip the Zodiacs. The captain decided to reposition us, take us farther down the Gerlache Strait to Paradise Harbour. Midmorning we got another departure time.

"Runners, RacingThePlanet runners—be prepared for 1 PM departure from the shell doors on Deck Three."

When the time came, I pulled on my bulky overcoat for warmth, my ship-provided knee-high muck boots, and threaded my life-preserver straps under my legs and cinched them into place. I put on my race pack and hand carried my drop bag. I was on the last Zodiac to arrive onshore.

I had only ten minutes to take off my muck boots, get my running shoes and Kahtoola Microspikes on, and be ready to run. The conditions were terrible, with wet, heavy snow falling to join the deep snow already on the ground. While I rushed to get situated, Hernan Garcia, the course director, briefed us in short, informational bursts. But there was really only one thing we cared to know: *How far?*

"It's a one-kilometer loop, and you will run counterclockwise."

Shit. Did he just say ONE kilometer? Safety, sure, but ONE fucking kilometer? We'll be right on everyone's heels!

There was no starter's pistol, no real start chute, and our group was a gaggle that looked less organized than a nearby penguin colony. It felt far less formal than the other races. Mary just counted backward and we lined up between the volunteers.

Mary shouted, "3, 2, 1 . . . GO!"

We headed uphill for half, downhill the other half. The first three laps were ridiculous. The snow wasn't hard packed and so everyone plunged into it up to midthigh. I fell at least a dozen times the first three laps. I wasn't the only one.

One fall was bad. I hit my left knee, the knee where I'd had one-third of the patellar tendon removed. It felt bruised. I also kept kicking my left foot's Microspike into my right ankle, which bled.

They saved the worst for last, I thought over and over. *This is fucking terrible.*

While Mary didn't outright say it, the first rule about running in Antarctica was you can't make yellow snow. That was a problem for me because that was how I checked my kidney function, by checking the color of my urine. Instead of just going anywhere, you had to run over beyond the start/finish down toward shore to the little open-air camp toilet. It was about a quarter mile one way. While not intentional, in effect, this was a time penalty for potty goers. Which meant I mostly held it in. No urine checks for kidney health this week.

The blowing wet snow was so thick I couldn't see much, but I could tell there were a couple guys ahead of me most of the day. One of them turned out to be Ben Dame, my German competitor, and we were arm's length from one another when we heard Mary yell out, "We're halting for the day." Ben and I finished the day tied for first.

Stage 1 on Antarctica, running through thick, wet snow.

It was 6 PM. We expected an 8 PM stop, but we ended early due to the conditions. I didn't know how many inches it snowed while we ran, but our drop bags were fully submerged when we got back to them.

November 26, 2022
Damoy Point

Nothing was certain. That was the tough thing about running on Antarctica. You got geared up and ready to go and then waved off—for hours at a time. We were supposed to depart on the Zodiacs at 2 pm, but the weather rolled in, and the dark sky suggested we wouldn't go at all.

But it cleared a little and we hit the landing site at 4 PM in hold-on-to-your-hat windy weather but at least with less snow falling than yesterday.

Today what looked like a megacolony of Gentoo penguins—thousands of them—surrounded the course.

Another punishing one. A two-kilometer loop on a sloped hillside. About half was uphill and half was downhill, and to add distance they built in star-tipped points marked in fluorescent ski poles poking out of the snow. The ins and outs felt like we were just running back and forth all day.

Before we started, Mary pulled us in. "We've got to keep you on an extra-tight leash today. There's blizzard weather in the area and we need to get back to the Zodiacs quick if it comes this way. Be prepared to run until 10 PM," she told us, but also, repeating her favorite phrase, reminded us, "Be prepared for anything." She gave us another down count: "3, 2, 1 . . . GO!" and we were off.

I started in third again and instantly noticed a pattern. Those first couple laps around were just brutal, plunging deep in soft snow. From my position I saw ahead to Ben. He was so light that he didn't seem to punch through the snow like I did. I would've sworn sometimes he looked like a German Jesus walking on snowy water.

The Gentoos, over time, migrated toward our race course. On one of the loops I ran up to see Szilvia—the women's leader and a Hungarian dentist—being attacked by an aggressive Gentoo, and Ahmed the cop from Abu Dhabi ran over to help shoo it off.

The wind was so strong I wore an extra shell. But it built up sweaty heat, and at the end my glacier goggles—wide-set to cover the entirety of my eyes from brightness—were fogged up so much I couldn't see the trail ahead. I was forced to drop my goggles for the last hour. The race doctors kept reminding us about the importance of eye protection for snow blindness (when the sun was out, it could reflect powerfully against the all-white backdrop). But at some point the immediate danger of a missed step and rolled ankle was worse than the risk to my eyes.

The thousands of penguins, the jagged icebergs, the smooth water, and the sharp white peaks were something movie magic couldn't cook up. But running forced me to spend the day looking only at my next step, which was frustrating.

I kept at it and over time, I broke ahead of Radmir the Russian and then even Ben. I took first and held that spot to the end.

Running with my Leader jersey on, Ben Dame just behind in pursuit.

We didn't get back until after 10 PM, then ate dinner at 10:45 PM and headed to bed by midnight. We thought we'd have another afternoon run tomorrow, but we didn't know for sure. Things changed quickly. I was tired.

While my brain was fried from focusing on each next step, what I did know was that I was now in the lead with 69 kilometers after two stages.

Ben was second with 67, Mori Mori in third with 66, Radmir had 64. As a red-blooded American, I did allow myself some small amount of pride in beating my German, Japanese, and Russian competitors. But only for a moment. There was still a long way to go.

November 27, 2022
Orne Island

We were in a rhythm. Breakfast 7 AM. Eleven AM race brief with departure time ("be prepared for anything"), no weather information ("be prepared for anything"), and no distance information ("be prepared for anything").

"RacingThePlanet runners," the announcement system blared. "Two-thirty PM at the shell doors on Deck Three."

Then we were held up by weather. Departure delayed. Another short-notice announcement told us we had thirty minutes. Race start 4 PM. Run until 9:30 PM. Dinner 10:30 PM.

The race course felt like we were in a big white rut, a 1.1-kilometer loop with star-pointed ins and outs again. With fifty runners, from above we must have looked like a giant game of Pac-Man, the faster runners gobbling up the slower ones.

The route would get packed in over time, but it was only a single person wide. So every step you made to the side was dangerous, as you didn't know if you'd punch through to your knee or if you'd hit a solid snow jackpot. All that dodging and plunging cost energy, not to mention the rolled-ankle risk. I took that risk hundreds and hundreds of times a day because to lead this race was to pass others that many times.

Sometimes passing actually provided some energy. Whenever I saw Ed or John or Julita or Elise on the course, after my standard "on your right" warning, we exchanged little cheers for one another. Mike, the Miami veterinarian, also became a great and positive supporter and went out of his way several times to encourage me onward. Every little bit helped.

The big news of the stage was that Mori Mori and I broke Ben's back. We put a full lap on him and Ben fell to third. The one question I had was whether Radmir could catch him, because that would throw Ben into fourth and make the 4 Deserts Champion trophy a possibility. At this point Radmir was down on Ben about six kilometers, which meant Radmir would have to lap Ben several times in the next few days.

Mori Mori, wearing his signature yellow hat, with Radmir close behind, and of course, our Gentoo penguin spectators in the foreground!

Can Radmir knock Ben out of third? Is it possible?

Just as important, I now had a five-kilometer lead on Mori Mori.

Can I hold off Mori Mori?

November 28, 2022
Danco Island

This is ugly.

Most days out there the course hardened over time as more feet packed the snow in. This day was different. It got wetter as the day went on, and the snow softened instead of becoming packed, which meant your feet punched through more as the day went on. It slowed me down. It slowed everyone down.

It was a 2.1-kilometer course, with a 300-foot slope, like a steep sledding hill. The huge hillside course looked like the outline of an upside-down Christmas tree, the pointy top at the start/finish area, switchbacks widening out and to the right as you went up, a long flat across the high point, and then winding zigzags back down and in back to the bottom.

Mori Mori and I tied, so I held my lead. Radmir and Ben tied with one fewer lap than Mori Mori and me. Radmir was running out of stages to catch Ben, but it was still a possibility.

For the past four days we'd run five hours a day, and now we had to make the transition from a late afternoon run on this day to an early morning race the next. We were briefed that tomorrow would be a 5 AM breakfast and 6:30 AM departure.

November 29, 2022
Petermann Island

This fifth stage was our most runnable so far, about 1.5 kilometers for the whole loop, with reasonably good weather, even some sun.

Leading Stage 5 in Antarctica.

There was nothing I could do to help Radmir. He was either going to outrun Ben or not. He could either get to a greater giddyap gear or not. My sole focus was to beat Mori Mori. That I could control.

Mori Mori and I got into this equilibrium today where I was half a lap up on him. We saw one another at the same point on the course all day, so we were both well aware of our positions relative to one another.

With an hour to go, I thought through our positions and pace, and I realized I had a chance to get in one last lap at the very end that he wouldn't be able to follow. The rules were that if you were beyond the start/finish when they called "stop" for the day, you were permitted to finish that lap. My goal was simple. Time it so I would be past the start/finish when "stop" was called and hope that Mori Mori couldn't keep up and would be forced to stop, so I would finish with one more lap on the stage than Mori Mori.

An hour passed, time wound down, and only a minute after I got my lap card punched and went through the start/finish, from behind I heard someone yell "STOP!"

I looked over my shoulder and saw Mori Mori come in to the finish. His legs slowed.

He stopped.

Yes! Yes! Yeah! He's done! I wanted to scream and laugh and pump my fists, but it wouldn't matter anyway because I knew I was running alone on a giant hunk of white at the bottom of the earth.

After five hours of running, when your trailer trails you like he's sharing your shoes, and you get that last lap in—it's an overwhelming feeling. Like a high-stakes game of last man standing, where I was the one still up.

But I was falling apart physically at this point. I kept having to drop my glacier goggles to see, so my eyes were ridiculously red from exposure to wind and snow. My legs were cement blocks, heavy and cracked all the way through.

When we finished, we had run for ten of the past twenty-one hours due to the switch from afternoon to morning stages. Mary told us we had a day off tomorrow.

It couldn't have come at a better time.

November 30, 2022
Gerlache Strait

The *Hondius* carried us north. The weather on the peninsula would be bad the next few days, so we headed to the South Shetland Islands with hopes for better weather.

On our day off, while the runners were offered the opportunity to do some of the tourist activities, like kayaking, I was in no condition for anything other than lying on my bunk.

I thought and napped. Napped and thought.

The year's events floated through my mind. My first race day was seven months ago. I started all this in the Namib Desert on May 1. The next day, on December 1, I would run the last one. Twenty-three stages down, one to go.

Back in the Namib I wouldn't have bet on myself to make it here. Never. And now here I was—one more morning, one more stage, one more race. The *Last* Desert.

This is it.

It wasn't just the feeling that I'd dodged dozens of bullets, lucky to have made it this far. It was that now I knew people were watching. They noticed. That message from Joey spun in my head: "You have had a huge influence on me."

I may be running in circles at the bottom of the earth, but there's a guy in Chicago who's gonna donate because I can still run those circles fast. This means something.

The stakes drove me to think worst case.

Mori Mori's performance at The Long March in the Atacama got in my head. We were so close, and then he just ran away with it. It reminded me of the six-day TransRockies Run in 2019. I had a twelve-minute lead on a guy after the first five stages. Somehow, on the twenty-three-mile final stage, he blew past me and finished so far ahead that he beat me by nearly two minutes overall. Even worse, when I ran in to the finish line, I heard the announcer call out his official victory—"Ladies and Gentlemen, in the biggest comeback in TransRockies history, Josh Ferenc of Vermont, representing Under Armour, has just defeated Matt Cavanaugh in the Open Men's Solo category."

To listen to yourself lose is a downer. I jogged in to the finish line a little over a minute later. It was awkward. The people in the finish area didn't know how to act around someone who'd blown up so bad.

Three years later, instead of that Under Armoured Vermonter, it was a yellow-hatted, North Face–wearing runner from Japan I worried about.

Mori Mori's so good he can just put the hammer down when he wants, I thought. *I can do everything right, run my legs off, and he just has that other gear. He's just better. Why even try when he can crush me?*

If he did the same thing he did in the Atacama during tomorrow's sixth stage—which he was clearly capable of—he could make the comeback. He could get back the seven kilometers he was down, especially as the stage was longer than any we'd had in this race. The potential for mistakes and fall downs and injuries dominated my mind. His comeback was possible. I knew. It had happened before. To me.

My strategy was simple: Keep him behind. No matter what. If I stayed ahead, I never had to worry. Forget every other runner. I couldn't do anything about Radmir or Ben. Besides, it wouldn't be too hard to keep track of Mori Mori's bright-yellow North Face hat, like being chased by a relentless traffic cone.

Tomorrow there would be nobody else but Mori Mori and me.

December 1, 2022
Deception Island
South Shetlands

This is it. Last day.

I pushed myself up from the bunk slowly, glanced at my watch.

Three AM. *Wow, time flies.*

I looked up at Ed, who looked back at me, grinning.

"Mornin', sunshine."

I grunted. Ed was mostly set to run.

One would think that after a down day my legs would be fresh. Instead, they were even stiffer, and I felt like I'd swapped my legs for two pegs. At least I got some more rest.

The ship didn't help. Overnight as we sailed, we left sheltered coves and went back into open-water swells that rolled the *Hondius* from side to side. I tried to get to sleep at 9 PM, but between then and the 3 AM wake-up, I didn't manage much.

Not long after I rubbed my eyes open, we sailed into Deception Island. Deception was as close as we'd get to British explorer Sir Ernest Shackleton's fateful 1914–1917 expedition. Shackleton's ship, *Endurance*, was caught in ice and later sank. His crew took refuge atop ice floes for months and then rowed three small boats north to Elephant Island in early 1916.

A century later and a little over a hundred miles west of Shackleton's route, the *Hondius* slid through a narrow opening known as "Neptune's Bellows."[41] A crew member told me the Russian captain would earn his pay here. I asked why.

"The Bellows can be tricky," he said. "There's a huge rock in the middle that's sunk many ships."

Deception wasn't a normal island. It was an active volcano—one of only a few in the world that ships can sail into. Deception was also a caldera, a previously blown-up volcano, which gave it a hollowed-out appearance. If you sat on a cloud, you could look down to see a giant C shape, a little over seven miles long and seven miles wide, where the C's two tips nearly touched at the end. To the island's east, at three o'clock, Mount Pond rose straight up out of the water to nearly 1,800 feet. From the inside of the C, you would get a panorama of black volcanic slopes, black sand beaches, and ash-coated glaciers.

A real-life Bond villain lair. I half expected Sean Connery or Daniel Craig to turn up.

Once beyond the Bellows, the C shape provided a sheltered harbor.

---

41 Named two hundred years ago by American seal hunters for the Roman sea god and the strong winds in the very narrow channel.

The winds calmed a little, and we sailed to our Deception Island landing site at Telefon Bay.

I left the cabin, walked down the hallway into the foyer, just before the loading area. John loitered there with Karen.

"You got this. Hold on for one more. You've got this," he said, which helped me push back the fears fluttering in my head.

We boarded the Zodiacs at 6 AM, bound for shore. The ship's tourists were bummed because they couldn't kayak. Even in the protected bay, the winds were too high for kayaks, about thirty miles per hour.

But we could still run. Mary gave us a quick race brief. We knew the drill by now.

"Today's loop is longer, 2.4 kilometers, and you'll find it's maybe our best of the week. You'll get to run more. We'll aim to be out here as long as we can to try to get the leaders their 250 kilometers, but as you all know, that will depend on the wind and the ship captain's decision. Be prepared to run until at least twelve noon. We're not sure when we'll have you stop, so be prepared for anything."

What she meant by "best of the week" was that the natural warmth from the volcano left about half the course, nearest the waterline, on black rock and sand. The other half, higher up from the water, was the familiar ice and snow we'd run in all week.

When Mary mentioned "the leaders," she meant me. I was at about 177 kilometers (about 110 miles), so to hit 250 I would have to run 73 kilometers (about 45 miles) today, over thirty laps.

As Mary finished, I pushed off my giant muck boots and pulled on my shoes, gaiters, and Kahtoola Microspikes. One string of thoughts passed through my mind over and over and over.

Not Atacama again. Not Mori Mori. Keep ahead.

We got our countdown, then started, running the loop counterclockwise. The start/finish was on the black sand near the water, the *Hondius* anchored offshore to our right as we came through for our lap card punches.

Running Stage 6, at Telefon Bay on Deception Island, with the *Hondius* in the background.

The loop began with a steady rise alongside a slanted hill, into the island's snowy interior, and then looped back with in- and outbound cuts. Those turns got tougher and tougher as the day went on, because the more tired the runners got, the harder it became to avoid the temptation to cut the course. With Mori Mori behind me, I didn't have that problem. I had someone watching me like a hawk every step.

I started in the lead. While most of the week I'd held back through the first and second laps—to let all the runners create a solid snowpack to run on—today I pushed out hard to signal to Mori Mori that I was strong.

For his part, he was always right there, close, never far back. So close sometimes I'd swear I could hear him breathing. In the history of hat wearing, nobody had ever despised one as much as I did that fucking yellow cap I just could not shake.

Much of the rest of the field was tired and done. So Mori Mori and I ran and chased, chased and ran, stuck together, pushing the pace for hours and hours. The left side of my neck got sore from looking back to check on him.

"Adam, is he there? Where's Mori?" I asked the race doctor, as he punched my ticket at the start/finish.

"Yeah, coming now. Maybe thirty seconds back," he responded.

It was like that all day.

We stayed rutted in that rhythm for hours when my second bottle started running out. The first bottle was bone dry. I knew it would be our longest stage, and I needed to be smart about fuel. I had a bottle at the start/finish race refuel point all set, pre-mixed with a blend of Tailwind Endurance Fuel and DripDrop, ready to go near my drop bag. The problem was I needed to take at least a full minute (more with a mistake) to get both empty bottles out of my chest harness, unscrew both caps, grab the big refuel bottle, unscrew its top, and then pour to refill both bottles. One minute at best, three minutes at worst.

I had built a decent gap since my last check-in. At this point Mori Mori was maybe two minutes back. A refuel stop was risky—unless I timed it to coincide with his own refuel stop. So I waited. I took fewer and fewer, smaller and smaller sips from the last bottle with liquid, and I nervously noted the expanding salt stains on my face and clothes. Just after I took the last sip from my second bottle, after I passed the race refuel point, I glanced back to see Mori Mori unscrew his bottle for a fill-up. Because I knew he ran with only one larger bottle, I calculated I would get a thirty-second or one-minute bump from his stop, enough cushion for my own stop.

I came in to the refuel area and mumbled to the volunteers, "Bottle, bottle."

I hustled to the designated tarp, found my refill bottle, and as my hands were frozen, an eager volunteer offered to help me refill.

"I got it," she said.

But it went wrong. In the exchange we fumbled the bottle onto the black sand. Some of my premixed refill spilled.

What might have taken a minute ended up taking longer. As I started to slide my second bottle back into my chest rig, there was Mori Mori charging toward me. I shoved my bottles down into place, dug my feet into the black sand, and pumped hard to get some space between us. It took work, but I managed to get ahead of him again.

One bottle empty, still moving on, holding off Mori Mori late during Stage 6.

Not long after, my refueling action generated a reaction. Now I needed to empty myself out.

It had been a joke for years between my brother Rob and me. Rob was never a runner, but he loved the stories about runners who came to marathon finish lines with legs coated in brown slurry. When I'd finish a race, he'd ask, "Did you *go* on yourself?"

I always said "no." Until Antarctica.

To go to the bathroom meant running off course toward the shoreline, then going to the bathroom, and then running back up to the course. That extra distance meant extra time that I didn't have with my yellow-hatted pursuer. Not to mention the hope that there wasn't a line of other runners at the time queuing up for the single toilet.

I looked back at Mori Mori. He was close. I didn't even really think about it, just more reacted to the circumstance. And then I did what I thought I would never do.

I emptied my bladder all the way into my many layers of cold-weather clothes. At first it bulged my wind briefs out, and then, because it couldn't penetrate the pants, the urine slowly leaked down my leg into my Gore-Tex shoes (they sealed *in* the liquid and wetted even my socks).

Warm for a flash. Then cold. A gross cold.

But I kept Mori Mori behind me. All costs meant all costs.

And then, when I felt like I was at the goal line, a huge problem crashed into me.

As I rounded the westernmost point on the course, about to pass Anim, the women's leader, she fell. She hit violently and hard onto a patch of solid rock exposed from the snowpack.

I had that world-slows-down-for-a-second moment.

I first thought: *Just let someone else help her. Someone will be here soon. Not my problem to solve.* Then: *Mori Mori still has time to catch me if something goes wrong—and this could be that something.*

What do I do?

Mori Mori was a couple minutes back. Even this late, my prime directive remained. But Anim's fall looked bad.

I stopped. I stopped, took a knee, looked for damage, started to put my hand under her arm to help her up.

I shouted through the wind: "Are you okay?"

Before she responded, I noticed something was wrong.

I touched my forehead. It was pure salt. My skin felt strange. I felt disoriented, like I was going to fall.

Maybe because I squatted down? Or was it from lifting her up? Maybe I'm too dehydrated? Or maybe I'm done. This is it.

I couldn't do anything and stood there frozen. I slowly stepped forward, the best I could do at this point. The fear set in. Here it was. The collapse. The fall. Mori Mori's comeback.

I was never going to win. I was always going to let him by. Destined to fail.

I felt like I was bleeding out. I looked down through the transparent case on my chest harness to see my daughters' blue blanket square. The weather had been so bad I'd encased it, hadn't touched it all week, but it had been there, within view, every step.

But now, maybe because I wasn't all there—all I could do was gaze at it.

I felt like I wasn't even there anymore, my mind drifted up like a balloon, above the snow, above the race, above the island.

A second system kicked on, the break-glass-in-case-of-emergency part of me.

Call it the runner's high or runner's low, spiritual transcendence, that holy fire I had after my donation—whatever it was shot images into my mind like a kaleidoscope of every warm memory in an otherwise unremarkable life.

I heard, "Daddy, I like to walk slow because I get to look at things." Georgie was five, reminding me not to rush through life, to hold on to good memories in my "brain pocket."

I saw Grace, the moment she tumbled into my hands and into the world.

I looked up from one knee to see Rachel smiling, on a balcony with beautiful mountain views, and she said, "Yes!"

I saw myself reading a message from a newly inspired donor, smiling, thinking: *Someone's gonna live.*

Then Mom, Dad, Rob, and Kevin, my entire unit from Iraq, even the guys killed in action. And somehow I felt my recipient, along with crowds of cameos of all the people who had sent in so much support when I needed it.

I felt connected to them all, there in my head. I knew it wasn't strictly real, but it felt as real as the penguins and icebergs. Through the cold, I warmed up. Then my little life movie paused, as a shout broke into my ear.

"Matt!" Anim's yell startled me.

She was still just steps behind me, yelling, "Go! Run! I'm okay! GO!" knowing how hard I had struggled to hold off Mori Mori all day. (We later learned the fall had broken her hand.[42])

I kept walking.

But then my walk quickened, then a slow jog, then a limping run. I was back.

I heard Mori Mori's footsteps on me now.

Still, I got to the next ticket punch in the lead. Each footstep felt like ten-times effort, like both legs were lead injected. But I kept going.

Sometimes, briefly, you can run on emotion alone. Sometimes, if you're lucky, you get so far past yourself you see running's truest beauty—that when you empty your body physically you can fill it spiritually, that when you trade something in your body you can get to something better in your soul.

I felt it all in the very same moment I realized it was over. I had helped another runner and *still* Mori Mori hadn't caught me.

By the time they called "last lap," my hands were immobile, frozen, discolored. Salty rivers slid past my eyes and nose. I didn't have to guess how close I was to being out of electrolytes; I saw the piles of white salt and empty bottles. I'd had sixty ounces of liquid to run over sixty kilometers (roughly thirty-seven miles).

"Finish! Finish!" I heard from volunteers clapping and smiling at the start/finish.

I crossed the line into a pack of a couple dozen volunteers and staff, with a roly-poly beached seal and a few hundred Gentoo penguins off to

---

42 After the race Anim wrote one of the kindest thank-you notes I have ever received: "It was an honor to be in the same race as you, you are a gentleman and a racer that exceed[s] all limits, thank you for picking me up when I fell face down, fractured hand and all you picked me up, shared your energy and gave me the power to continue, you are my hero and trust me I don't have many."

our right. I walked to where they were handing out finishers' medals, but Telefon Bay was now so windy that we couldn't really celebrate. Often at RacingThePlanet finishes, someone hands you your country's flag to hold up overhead, but the wind made that impossible.

Just after crossing the finish line to win The Last Desert on Antarctica.

Mary shouted, "Alright, Matt!" as race photographer Thiago Diz and videographer Michael Murphy looked on and recorded the moment.

"I don't know if I can stand much longer," I said weakly.

She asked, "How does it feel?"

Even weaker, I responded, "It feels good, it feels really good."

"What do you want to do *now*?" (Mary teed up the *Are-you-gonna-go-to-Disney World!?* prompt.)

I was far too drained to give a creative response.

"I want to go home now."

I also grinned a little, because I still had all those people in my mind from that cloudy moment on the course. But Mary didn't know that, so I'm sure to her I had just delivered the lamest-ever response to that question.

In my defense, I had nothing left. Nothing more to give. Nothing.

The winds picked up, and the staff hustled us out to the Zodiacs for the choppiest, wettest ride back to the ship of the entire week.

It was over. It was finally, really over.

I won.

On the ship, I learned Mori Mori and I tied on the stage with 60 kilometers each. The Last Desert final tally in the Men's competition: Radmir, 207 kilometers; Ben, 218.7 kilometers; Mori Mori, 230 kilometers; I finished with 236.7 kilometers.

Aboard the *Hondius* with Mori Mori and Ben Dame and our Top Three finisher medals.

I lost the 4 Deserts Champion trophy to Ben Dame. He finished with 10 points, I had 11, and Mori Mori had 12.

I was disappointed but so beat up it was impossible to muster the energy to be angry. There was a silver lining though—RacingThePlanet officials informed me afterward that I had finished as the fastest American ever to race the 4 Deserts series, Grand Slam or otherwise, by a large margin. I also learned that in RacingThePlanet's twenty years, over 10,000 runners from 100-plus countries had finished an event. Under 300 had joined the 4 Deserts Club by finishing all four deserts over several years, in a series that *Time* magazine had twice counted among the toughest endurance races in the world, alongside the Tour de France. At the time, about eighty competitors had completed all four in under one year to earn the Grand Slam title (in addition to joining the 4 Deserts Club).

In the end, I was the first kidney donor to Grand Slam the 4 Deserts, won The Last Desert in Antarctica, came within a single point of winning the 4 Deserts Champion trophy in the closest finish in race history, and, importantly, set that record as the fastest American to ever race the 4 Deserts.

But all that—all of it—paled in comparison to the thirteen words Rachel typed into social media after the final stage. She wrote, "Not only did he win Stage 6, he won the whole damn thing!"

Rachel's proud of me, I thought, *really proud of me. That makes everything better.*

ACTION THIS DAY

Most wars are won by attrition. Simply outlasting the other side. Nothing fancy, nothing clever—just outenduring the adversary.

Antarctic explorer Ernest Shackleton's family motto was "Through endurance we conquer." The *Hondius* had signs and postcards everywhere with the expression. You couldn't walk the ship without a reminder.

It was useful because endurance is often overlooked by its cousin, courage. But courage is fleeting, endurance is forevermore.

Courage is the tide—endurance, the rocky shore. They are related but not the same. Endurance is long-run courage, courage married to a vision that sees beyond the moment for resolve on the road to some better victory. Endurance's most important and persistent question is "What next?" It cares less about today's result and more about tomorrow's try; it is relentless optimism in the blackest of bleak circumstances, fundamentally future oriented.

Of the ten lessons listed in this book so far, this is the most important. The good news is that we can expand our "endurability"—our capacity to endure—through acts of radical generosity and always knowing who and what we're fighting for. This principle, this idea, that we can actually build up our endurability is in itself hope in the hardest circumstances.

And we need that hope because in-the-moment endurance rarely looks pretty. Anything but. It's horrible. That's the point. Just as there is no courage without fear, there is no endurance without weakness. And weakness will show, inevitably, in the doing of the hard thing.

But endurance shows up. Because as Shackleton pointed out, it is through endurance—and endurance alone—that we conquer. Our fears, our adversaries, ourselves: To endure is the most important quality.

Even when our courage fails, we can still endure.

Is there a challenge in your life you might overcome through endurance?

Epilogue

BEST SCAR WINS

If we let them, our scars can be our best stories and most profound strength.

December 10, 2023
Honolulu, Hawaii

In 2023, I served as the CEO and president of the National Kidney Donation Organization, and we needed a new way to find people interested in kidney donation. So the year after 1K4D, I tried 1K12—a dozen major marathons, all under three hours, all in cities with major transplant centers. Atlanta; Los Angeles; Salt Lake City; Cincinnati (Flying Pig); Denver (Colfax); San Diego; Twin Cities; Hartford; Washington, DC (Marine Corps); New York City; and Philadelphia. Coached by John Bezou, I made it through those first eleven big-city marathons and averaged 2 hours, 54 minutes (by my GPS watch). I made it through training in Utah's winter straight to racing in hot cities like Atlanta and Los Angeles. I made it through a torn adductor tendon that pulled partially off my pubic bone. I made it through a stretch of four marathons in five weeks.[43] I made it all the way to eleven for eleven.

Then I met my Waterloo in Honolulu.

As I lay on a stretcher in Kapiʻolani Park, next to the finish line at the Honolulu Marathon, all I could think was: *I didn't make it in time.*

By three minutes. I lost. Three minutes late.

The hot, salty breeze from Waikiki Beach wasn't strong enough to cool my overheated body down on that stretcher, so after finishing I found myself cared for by a doctor who had previously worked as medical staff at RacingThePlanet events (what a tiny world we live in).

The Honolulu Marathon had started at 5 AM in the mid-eighty-degree Fahrenheit range, with over 90 percent humidity, and it got worse over the morning. In a year of racing over 300 miles, it all collapsed in the last three miles. I lost a minute per mile over the final three miles and finished three minutes over my three-hour goal.

That left a scar.

1K12 wasn't all loss. It reached millions of Americans through seventy-four minutes of television in major media markets across the country, as well as social media and print publications that covered the races, and boosted NKDO's fundraising significantly. I qualified for the Boston Marathon a dozen times. So there was still some success in that final failure.

---

43 The Twin Cities Marathon was cancelled that year; I did a makeup near home in Park City, Utah, at 7,000 feet elevation. My 1K12 partner was the supermom-warrior-triathlete-teacher Hilary Baude, also a kidney donor. She not only did the dozen marathons, but two of her marathons came during Ironman events. We were both supported by our photographer and friend, fellow kidney donor, one of the best human beings on the planet, Steve Wilson.

Beyond that, sometimes it takes a finish line to look back and reflect on a race's true meaning. *What was it all about?*

I'm at that point now. It's taken a while to process, frankly in part because Rachel and I didn't make it. We've split up, amicably, though still painfully (another scar), and have taken our first steps toward new and different lives. *What happened?* you might wonder. That makes two of us, because if I'm completely honest, I don't fully know. Sometimes it's impossible to see truth even from the inside. What I do know with certainty, what has remained unchanged, is our joint commitment to parenting two wonderful girls.

Which begs the question—why listen to me? The self-help industrial complex is alive and well and, at this point in the book, I'm supposed to put my hands on my hips, stand as the Man of Steel, and reveal some tip, tool, or trick that makes you into one too. Or pitch you an unscientific, gimmicky self-care routine—a diet, cleanse, microdose, or meditation—that promises to make you 11 percent better. I should present myself as a guru, invincible, even a hero.

You know I'm not. I told you from the get-go and you've seen along the way—I'm not great or good, even if I desperately want to be. You know I've lost races I should've won. You know I've picked stupid fights with my mom. You know I've felt real failure as a father. You know I'm working my way past a divorce. You know I've got regrets, more than a few, and that if you took a drink each time I've cried or defecated on myself in this story, you'd now be too drunk to finish the last few pages.

And still.

If you can set those imperfections aside, and I hope you can, you might listen to me because you know I'm not selling anything other than the power in an act of radical generosity.

So far I've told you the "how," the ten lessons, the compass I used on this journey. Now I owe you the "why," some thoughts on my North Star, because a how needs a why like a body needs a soul.

I know radical generosity works because I've been on both sides—the helped and the helper. I've run out of bullets and got to fire a silver bullet. My mission now is to show people that they too have a silver bullet. "A life is not important except in the impact it has on other lives" is etched on groundbreaking baseball player Jackie Robinson's tombstone. When we give more, we live more.

We all have that silver bullet. We do. For some great purpose, whatever that purpose might be. And if we fire it, our lives get better when we help someone in dire need. The greatest gift is to bear another person's pain without breaking ourselves. To endure that is what makes us great.

The good news is that radical generosity has a boomerang effect. Just as it benefits the recipient, it reflects back on the giver in other ways. My kidney recipient gave me a great gift—the opportunity to do something unambiguously good for another. And that has improved my life emotionally at least as much as theirs physically.

The same dual nature applies to scars. A yin and yang. Everyone has them. And we should be proud of them.

Too often we see only the downside and not the upside.[44] We remember the moment of impact, the scream when the skin sliced, the second we heard the bone go "crack." That sound gets stuck in our heads. The same is true with the other awful things that happen to us—deaths, divorces, firings, the things that cause floods of tears that can't be contained even with our own Hoover Dam.

But these tough experiences equally represent the most profound part of being human—we can build back better. Bones and hearts break and can heal back stronger. Break a car and it won't mend itself, but we can. And we do this work on a regular basis. It's not instant, but it's a miracle nonetheless. During my year of running through deserts, I learned to take more and more pride in my own scars, realizing that they were the driving

---

44 Of course, some scars require real help and support from others to bear.

force behind my donation and all that's followed. Remember: *Dolor hic tibi proderit olim—someday this pain will be useful to you.*

A scar is just a spot where you've grown more than others. I have plenty. I listed some of the emotional ones already. Physically, there are too many to list in full, but here are some: the big one on my left knee where they took one-third of my patellar tendon; right ankle extending up my leg from a bad break requiring a titanium plate and screws; the medium-sized ones on my forehead, my chin, and the top of my head; there's the one on my right forearm where my brother Rob stabbed me with a kid's prison shank (a sharp piece of plastic); and on my left forearm the patch of regrown skin over the place I slid headfirst into artificial turf while playing baseball.

Then there are my best ones. From the kidney surgery I have four small sideways slits running up and down the left side of my abdomen like a little ladder. Below my navel and to my right side I have that horizontal scar that runs the length of a pointer finger where they took my kidney out. From the races I have three or four white blotches on my back where the skin rubbed off under the weight of my race pack.

I'm proud of them all, these more recent arrivals the most. If we let them, our scars can be our best stories and most profound strength. A renewable resource we can use for endurance when there seems little cause to endure.

What makes the strength in our scars?

Every scar is a lesson. The toughest lesson. The hardest lesson. The best lesson. A lesson you never forget. And when you add those up, they make a good reference point for growth. I've found every way to fall physically and athletically, and it literally shows on my body. Maybe winners are just the losers who learn from their lumps. Scars help us get there.

Scars bind us to others. To humanity—to strangers, to friends and family alike. They are the something that we know, without a doubt, we all carry in common. If we want to know someone, connect deeply, we can do worse than to start with their scars.

Scars are our history, written in hieroglyphics, etched into our bodies. They're pictures of what we've overcome to be here, today, now. They make us unique, one of a kind. They show that we've tried, we've lived, and sometimes, we've even dared greatly, with the nicks and cuts to prove it.

But we heal. We move on. We grow past. And that healing process is our superpower. We're not invincible, but give us enough time and we'll bounce back from almost anything. Like slow-motion Wolverines (minus the adamantium).[45] Scars show us this.

This process of physical regeneration and spiritual renewal comes down to three words.

Best scar wins.

Best scar wins. Those three pack a lot in. Above all, they recognize the world's going to leave its mark on us, and that we're resolved to leave our mark on the world. We will be scarred, but those scars can give birth to greater wins. Nothing great or good comes without cost. The question is *if*—and *what*—we're willing to pay.

Best scar wins is permission to accept our flaws and scars, because none of us is either perfect or getting through life unscathed. Our best scars are strength not weakness, power not pain.

Best scar wins leverages that strength for selfless ambition. Our best wins transcend place or podium, meaning that when we give beyond ourselves, we can push beyond ourselves to where the successes are superior and the losses are less. The best way to get ahead may be to give ahead.

Best scar wins is a virtuous cycle. Suffering leaves scars. Scars give strength. Strength to relieve suffering. Your scar may ultimately become someone's cure.

It took me a wild year's worth of blood and toil, loss and win to truly understand that radical generosity isn't merely about what you give up, what you subtract from yourself—but what you can gain, and that those

45 Hugh Jackman, *the* Wolverine, if you're reading this, get in touch. Kidney donation could use your help in getting the word out. I'd even take a Ryan Reynolds (*Deadpool*).

gains can add up to an even larger life. I hope you take these lessons, along with the others in this book, and grow to be more than you were before. I did.

Because life will continue to throw obstacles onto the trail, and we'll just keep using those lessons, working our way through, problem by problem, until we get to the next challenge that others see as unbearable, unattainable, unimaginable. And when those doubters present themselves, announce their doubts in person—we'll think, *Let's do this*, and then respond with three undeniably powerful words:

Best scar wins.

For Potential Kidney Donors

If you are considering becoming a living kidney donor, here's what you need to know about the process:

Getting started: Register online as a potential donor using the QR code on page 216.

Testing: Once you have registered, you'll provide a comprehensive medical history and undergo several tests, such as blood tests, a CT scan, an MRI, etc. If you are approved, you will have surgery to remove your kidney.

Recovery: Most people will be in the hospital for one to three days and can return to normal activities after two to four weeks. Kidney donors do not have to take any medications or make any significant changes to their diets, lifestyles, or activities postdonation.

Risks: Kidney donation is a very safe and low-risk surgery, and studies have shown that kidney donation does not significantly affect a donor's long-term health. Donors typically lead healthy lives and have life expectancies comparable to nondonors.

Matching: If you donate through the National Kidney Registry, you do not have to be a biological match for your intended recipient. If you are not a match, or not a very good match, the NKR will find a match for your kidney, and your donation will generate a voucher. This voucher allows your intended recipient to receive a living kidney-donor transplant from a compatible donor in the future.

Costs: Donating a kidney should not cost you anything. The medical expenses associated with kidney donation are generally covered by the recipient's insurance. Nonmedical costs incurred by the donor, such as lost wages, travel, and childcare, can be covered by Donor Shield, but all donors should double-check with their transplant coordinator to make sure they are enrolled in Donor Shield.

More questions? Visit www.kidneyregistry.com/for-donors.

Register now:

Acknowledgments

You know those classic space shuttle takeoff scenes? The ones where a whole Mission Control's worth of people huddle together in a big room?

That's what it took to get this book to blast off, and it'll take a minute to go row by row, section by section, through my Mission Control, to name and thank and praise everyone who helped make this dream a reality. (Of course, I won't be able to get to everyone in such a short space, so please visit BestScarWins.com for a far fuller list of acknowledgments.)

It starts with you. Yes, you. The one reading this now, like, reading these very words. The easiest thing to do in the world is to stop reading, to put the book down and pick up the smartphone. Thanks for coming on board for this bumpy ride, and if you can, please let someone—maybe even me—know what you thought of the story.

For a book to be born, someone first has to conceive of the idea, but then a lot of others—a whole lot—have to help get it out into the world.

Scott Perry, my favorite runner-slash-agent, you believed in this book before it even became a book. Thank you to everyone at Matt Holt Books and BenBella, especially Katie Dickman and Scott Calamar. Beth Downing, David Krissman, Mary Cate Wilhelm, and Sam Fanshawe: Your reading, reviewing, and suggestions were all far more than generous. They made the book what it is. You're the best.

I've never, ever bought a lottery ticket because I know I won the best lottery there is to be born into my family (Mom, Dad, Rob, Kevin, and all the other Cavanaughs out there). You always offered support and your opinions—and then had the wisdom and restraint to let me chart my own course (even when you knew I was skydiving without a parachute). It's made all the difference, thank you.

To Grace and Georgie: *Moibe! Moibesans!* It will probably be difficult for you to respect a father who's written a book in which he pees on himself—but do try, try very hard. You should know that little blue scrap of your baby blanket was with me every step, that you, in some small way, were with me every step, especially the hard ones, especially the bad ones. My heart and soul and legs are stronger for your presence in my life.

For Rachel: Thank you for your support and for being a fantastic mom. I never meant for things to turn out as they have, and I am deeply sorry that they have. But all finish lines are start lines, and I wish you the best as the next pistol fires. I know you'll run well. (You'll have to in order to keep up with the two *Moibesans.*)

My final thank-you is the most important one. To my recipient. You gave me the greatest gift, the opportunity for genuine generosity, the opportunity to be useful to another, the opportunity for one virtuous act in an imperfect life. Thank you. Thank you. Thank you.

About the Author

ML (Matt) Cavanaugh, PhD, is a retired lieutenant colonel and US Army strategist who earned two Bronze Star Medals and the Combat Action Badge for his time in the Iraq War. A proud living kidney donor, he most recently served as president and chief executive officer of the National Kidney Donation Organization. Matt, a 2002 West Point graduate, co-founded the Modern War Institute at West Point; has been the youngest recipient of the Army Strategist Association's professional award, the Order of Saint Gabriel the Archangel; earned acclaim as the top professor at West Point; and was once named the US Army Athlete of the Year. A contributor to the *Los Angeles Times*, Matt's writing has also been featured in outlets including the *New York Times*, *Washington Post*, *Wall Street Journal*, *USA Today*, and the *Sydney Morning Herald*. As a sought-after public and motivational speaker based in Colorado, Matt has shared insights with large and small companies, medical and healthcare organizations, sports teams, and students across the country. For more, please visit MLCavanaugh.com or BestScarWins.com.